THE MAGIC OF HERBS

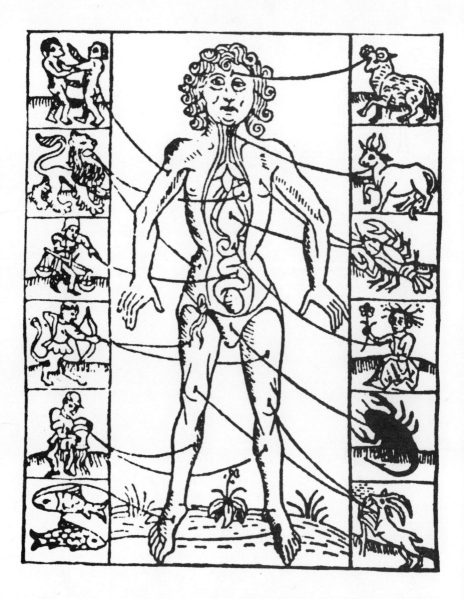

From a German incunabulum of 1484. The picture illustrates the connections of the different signs of the zodiac with the human body.

THE MAGIC OF

DAVID CONWAY

E. P. DUTTON & CO., INC.

NEW YORK 1973

Library of Congress Catalog Card Number: 73-79539
SBN: 0-525-15025-0

PRINTED AND BOUND IN GREAT BRITAIN

CONTENTS

INTRODUCTION

I WAS FOUR years old when I discovered the medicinal use of herbs. Suspected of having caught worms from the family cat, I was made to drink a brew composed of broom, bilberry leaves and wormwood. (The cat was spared the medicine and left to harbour worms in peace.) From then on throughout my childhood I was dosed with other herbs whenever illness threatened. Their taste was rarely pleasant, but at least they worked. So well, in fact, that at an early age I resolved to learn all I could about them.

Here I was fortunate, because we then lived in a rural part of Wales where people trusted herbs more than they did the modern drugs prescribed by doctors. And among the herbal experts people went to see was a good friend of my father's, a widower named Mr James, Tan'rallt.

Mr James kept a farm on Plynlimon, a desolate range of hills just east of Aberystwyth. To my young eyes he seemed a larger than life character: tall, enormously stout and clad always in brown tweed, he had what my mother claimed was the foulest tongue in Wales. When he spoke in her presence, she invariably put her hand across her mouth, as if willing him to close his own. Once I asked her why she never put her hands over her ears, which seemed more appropriate in the circumstances. 'That would be rude,' she replied, 'and besides, I'd miss what he was saying.'

And this was the point, for among the oaths and imprecations there was wisdom to be found. Here was a man who knew the countryside and all its secrets. People from neighbouring farms consulted him whenever they or their animals were ill, for he knew which plants to prescribe for everything from colic to the evil eye. Indeed, his knowledge of plants was extraordinary, although he probably knew the names of not more than half a dozen. But whereas any botanist might tell you that the lesser celandine was a member of the Ranunculaceae family and the possessor of three sepals and numerous stamens, my father's friend knew that this plant was ruled by Mars and provided in its root a sovereign remedy for piles and other rectal disorders. (Not that the foulest tongue in Wales would have put it quite as delicately as that.)

From Mr James I learned most of what I now know about the use of herbs. He himself inherited this knowledge from his father, who in turn acquired it from his own father before him. Three or four generations previously the James family had lived in Carmarthenshire, and Mr James's proudest boast was that he was a direct descendant of the great Welsh herbal doctors known as *Meddygion Myddfai*.

An explanation is required here, for these Myddfai doctors are not known widely outside Wales, and, ultimately, it is their herbal learning that permeates this book.

Their story starts nearly eight hundred years ago on a farm near the village of Llanddeusant, where there lived a widow and her only son, Gwyn. Every morning the young man drove his mother's cattle up the Black Mountain, where ample pasture could be found. One day, as the cows were grazing by a lake called Llyn-y-Fan Fach, Gwyn saw at the water's edge a maiden so beautiful that he fell in love with her at once. For want of something better to say he offered her a little bread and cheese, but, laughing, she declined his food and dived into the lake. Only then did it dawn on Gwyn that this woman was a nymph.

Back home the boy's mother listened to his story and suggested that on the next encounter he should offer unbaked bread to his fairy sweetheart. This he did, and at the same time begged her to marry him. But she refused, saying, 'Your bread is unbaked. For that reason I shall not have you.'

After this Gwyn and his mother hit upon a compromise, and when the nymph appeared next the bread he had to offer was half baked. With it went the same proposal of marriage which, to his delight, the girl accepted, subject to one condition. This was that she would

8

leave him if he struck her three times. Gwyn readily agreed to this condition, whereupon the nymph, whose name was Nelferch, dived into the water, reappearing seconds later with another nymph, her double, and a dignified old man.

The old man, father of both girls, said he would approve the match provided Gwyn could distinguish Nelferch from her sister. This our young hero succeeded in doing, having noticed that Nelferch's sandals were fastened differently from those of her twin. The wedding thus took place and, as her dowry, Nelferch brought with her from the lake all the cows she could count in one breath. Soon afterwards she and her new husband made their home in Esgair Llaethwy, a farm not far from the hamlet of Myddfai, some six miles north of Llyn-y-Fan. Here three sons were born to them.

One morning years later, when Gwyn and his wife were on their way to visit friends, Nelferch complained of tiredness. Her husband thereupon suggested that she should catch a horse from the next field while he ran home to fetch some reins. When he returned, Nelferch was still standing where he had left her and Gwyn gave her a gentle tap on the shoulder. Thus was struck the first blow. The second followed some years later, when Nelferch began crying at a wedding. Again it was no more than a tap, but the damage was done. The third and last blow occurred at a funeral, when Nelferch burst into hysterical laughter, and her husband, to bring her to her senses, slapped her on the cheek. Sadly she said farewell to him, kissed her three sons, now grown to manhood, and returned with her dowry to the depths of Llyn-y-Fan.

Only once did Nelferch reappear from beneath the lake, and that was to her eldest son, Rhiwallon. To him she disclosed that he and all his male descendants would become physicians, and to launch him on his new career, she gave him a sack of herbs and advice on how to use them.

This story of the lady from the lake may or may not be true. What cannot be denied is that there exists a thirteenth-century manual written in Welsh which contains up to nine hundred herbal recipes, many of which are described in the pages that follow. All nine hundred are alleged to be the work of Rhiwallon and his three sons, Cadwgan, Gruffydd and Einion. These, then, were the original physicians of Myddfai, and it is their successors who have practised herbalism for centuries in Wales. One of the last of them was a certain Rhys ap Williams of Aberystwyth, who died in 1842 and who, the story goes, was a relation of my father's friend Ifor James, Tan'rallt.

Tan'rallt Farm – the name means 'Below the Hill' – was situated in a mountain valley, too high and too bleak for anything other than sheep-farming. Along one side the Forestry Commission had seen fit to plant some fir trees, but few had managed to survive. Otherwise nothing much grew there except grass and a protective clump of alders near the house. This whitewashed building, together with some ramshackle outhouses, can still be seen from the road that crosses Eisteddfa Gurig on its way to Ponterwyd and thence to Aberystwyth. By now, however, the house lies empty and its roof, I am told, has fallen in.

Despite his wonder-working reputation, Mr James was not a prosperous man. Or, if he was, he never showed it. On entering his house one passed into a murky darkness which two little windows strove in vain to lighten. Gradually, as one's eyes grew accustomed to the shade, one observed the squalor all around. Downstairs – I never saw the loft – a large room served as living-room and kitchen, but only a tiny space around the range was habitable, the rest being filled with rubbish. Here, old harness, rusting shot-guns and a spade or two could usually be discerned among the stacks of peat and piles of *Farmers Weekly*'s. And, of course, above one's head there hung the herbs, great bunches of broom, loosestrife, sage and comfrey, all drying in their own sweet time.

In this room, seated on the settle, I watched old Mr James prepare and mix his herbs. For Mrs Price, the Post, who suffered from the dropsy, a pinch of larkspur, two of nettle and a good handful of tansy, the lot to be infused in water and taken three times daily. For old Moses Jones's cough, a mixture of coltsfoot, liquorice and honey. And as a pick-me-up for Lizzie Hughes, some yarrow and a little rue to be swallowed in a glass of milk at eleven o'clock each morning. And all the time Mr James would tell me what he was preparing, and why he chose one herb in preference to another. There was much for a young lad like myself to learn, but my teacher was a good one.

In this book you can join me on that settle and together we can learn the ancient lore of herbs. For none of what now follows is my own invention; it is simply what I learned from a remarkable old man.

Nor was it his invention, either, since, as we have just seen, it belongs to a rich tradition stretching back to the legendary Myddfai doctors and, perhaps, through them, to Nelferch, nymph of Llyn-y-Fan. Such ancestry is appropriate, for herbs have something truly magical about them. And, of course, they work!

The preparation of medicinal herbs. From a twelfth-century copy of the
Herbarium of Apuleius

I

BOTANICAL MEDICINE

HERBALISM IS the earliest form of medicine. In Man, the knowledge that plants can cure disease is probably instinctive, for even animals seek out the appropriate herb whenever they are ill. For thousands of years medicine depended almost exclusively on flowers, barks and leaves; only recently have synthetic drugs come into use, and in many cases these are carbon copies of chemicals identified in plants. Even now in the twentieth century pharmaceutical firms sponsor expeditions to remote parts of the world in search of medicinal plants, just as in 1500 B.C. Queen Hatsheput of Egypt sent court botanists on missions of this sort. The fact is that modern science has amply vindicated the instinctive confidence the ancients placed in herbs.

The study and use of plants for medicinal purposes is the concern of herbalism. It is no less the concern of orthodox medicine, which puts equal faith in the curative value of certain plants. And yet, although the continued use of plant remedies in standard medical practice proves the worth of herbal therapy, herbalism itself is normally regarded as a quaint aberration fit only for quacks, fools and hypochondriacs. From the outset, therefore, we had better ask ourselves in what way herbalism differs from respectable pharmacology.

The answer herbalists would give is that their method is more 'natural' than that followed by their rivals. They imply, like health-food addicts, that natural somehow equals good – a dubious implication, if only because of the difficulty in deciding what is natural and what is not. After all, a herbalist who grubs about in hedges is really no more natural than a chemist at work in his laboratory. Nor are the botanical infusions of the one necessarily any better than the medicines of the other: both are natural and both probably do good.

In my view, herbal medicines are more natural only in the sense that their preparation is less complicated than that of modern drugs. In herbalism a plant is simply eaten raw or else infused in water. In orthodox medicine, on the other hand, the same plant may be subjected to umpteen chemical processes before its active ingredient is extracted, refined and made ready for consumption. Instead of more natural, therefore, we should perhaps say that herbalism is the cruder method of the two.

The advantage of the orthodox method is that it identifies and so employs only the beneficial part of each particular plant. (This substance may then be copied in order to produce a synthetic alternative that is cheaper and more readily available.) Another advantage is that the active ingredient can be administered in concentrated form, thus ensuring that it acts quickly and with maximum effect. But this has its disadvantages as well. The trouble is that by their swift and certain action drugs can cure illness without requiring more from the body than the correct physiological responses. As a result, the patient's co-operation in his own treatment is kept to a minimum.

Herbs, on the other hand, achieve results more slowly, and in the time they take the body has a chance to help them in their fight to cure its ills. Thanks to such collaboration, the body does not lose – from want of practice – its natural ability to heal itself. In this way, too, it builds up its resistance to disease* and learns how to cope with sickness on those occasions when herbs or other medicines are unavailable.

Apart from these differences in method, the development of medicine itself helps us to understand why herbalism is relegated to its outer fringes. The earliest physicians were all herbalists and one of these, Hippocrates, has left a valuable description of the herbs in use throughout the classical world. Many of these are still popular today, among them balm, basil, horehound, ivy, rue and sage. Other major figures such as Galen and Celsus were likewise fond of herbal simples, but the ancient doctor most committed to them was Dioscorides who, in

---

* Unlike what happens when virus diseases are treated with modern antibiotic drugs. Here the virus builds up resistance to the drug while the body stays as vulnerable as ever.

the first century of our era, produced a *materia medica* in which over five hundred plants are mentioned.

In medieval Europe the practice of medicine was undertaken by religious orders, some of whose hospitals and herb gardens can still be seen today. So too can the illuminated herbals produced around this time, in which virtuous plants are catalogued, and beautifully – if over-imaginatively – drawn. More herbals began to appear once printing was invented, their illustrations conforming more closely with the appearance of the plants they described. These early herbals enjoyed considerable success and included not only reissues of antique works like that of the Greek Apuleius Platonicus, but originals like the famous *Ortus Sanitatis* or the great *Herbal* of William Turner, a man who has been called the Father of English botany.

The circulation of these herbals enabled those who could read to indulge in self-medication when they felt in need of it. The poor had been doing this all along, relying on a fund of herbal lore handed down from one generation to the next. For, unlike other forms of medicine, herbalism required no special skills or expensive apparatus: provided the patient knew which plant best suited his condition, he had only to obtain it from the hedgerow. It was easy, it cost nothing and it worked.

Here, then, was a form of therapy that was recognized by science but could be applied by those who lacked any scientific training. There thus came into being two sorts of 'green' medicine, the one carried on by qualified physicians as part of general medical practice, the other left to men and women with no formal training. Each developed more or less independently of the other, the name 'herbalism' being used to distinguish the activity of the amateurs.

The gulf between herbalism and orthodox medicine has since widened, the rapid advances of the latter seeming to make obsolete all rival forms of treatment. But these advances have in many cases been due to knowledge stolen from other sources, and herbalism, though overtly despised, has been plundered more than most.

Thus, cancer researchers, taking the hint from herbalists as far back as Pliny the Elder, who recommended mistletoe for treating cancer, have found that its juice does indeed produce 50 per cent tumour inhibition in some experimental mice. Similar results have been noted from administering extracts of garlic and bloodroot, two

15

plants traditionally used in herbalism to treat cancerous conditions.*
These results do not, of course, mean that herbalists know how to
cure cancer, but they do indicate that they were not wholly misguided
in the plant remedies they prescribed.

Nor can science afford to fault many other herbalist prescriptions:
wormwood is a traditional cure for worms, and from it pharmacists
now obtain the vermifugal drug santonin (just as pyrethrum is
extracted from wormwood's cousin, the chrysanthemum); the tranquillizing drug reserpine, widely used on the mentally sick, was
discovered through observing the success Indian herbalists had in
treating madness with a plant called snakeroot (*Rauwolfia serpentina*).
But the classic case is the discovery in the eighteenth century of
digitalin, the active ingredient in foxgloves. This came about because
a young Midlands doctor, William Withering, chanced to hear how
foxglove tea brewed by a Shropshire farmer's wife had removed
dropsical symptoms caused by cardiac malfunctioning. Dr Withering's
own experiments confirmed the plant's worth as a heart tonic, something herbalists in and out of Shropshire had known since the time
of Dioscorides. It was then left to another medical man, Dr Erasmus
Darwin, grandfather of Charles, to publish an account of the foxglove's
merits, and, before long, it became an accepted cardiac treatment,
tablets from its powdered leaves still being prescribed today.†

So far we have seen that what distinguishes herbalism from orthodox
medicine are its simpler methods and the lack of formal medical
training among those who practise it. We have seen, too, that these
characteristics do not render it invalid. On the contrary, past experience suggests that science may still have much to learn from the
corpus of herbal knowledge we possess. Every day, cures – some of
them little short of amazing – are attributed to the use of herbs, and
here, of course, is the real test of their worth. It is a test which readers
of this book can try out for themselves.

---

* Further details of research in this field will be found in B. Krieg, *Green Medicine*
(London, Harrap, 1965), pp. 299 *et seq.*

† Digitalis is now known to stimulate the vagus centre, the cranial nerve that monitors
the heart's activity. Because its effect varies from person to person, few modern
herbalists prescribe foxglove. Instead, they prefer hawthorn or lily-of-the-valley.
The latter has now been found to contain a digitalis-type drug to which the name
convallotoxin has been given.

Before then, however, there are two more aspects of herbalism to be considered. They provide, I am afraid, two further reasons why herbalism has fallen into disrepute. Not content with merely using herbs, our ancestors sought to philosophize about them, inventing theories to explain why a particular plant cured the disease it did. For a long time astrological reasons were given to explain the different actions of various herbs. When reading about them, however, you should bear in mind that in medicine results alone count – and, as you will discover, herbs give the results expected of them, astrology notwithstanding.

CHRYSANTHEMUM

NICHOLAS CULPEPER. From the second edition of *A Physicall Directory* (1650)

2
HERBALISM AND ASTROLOGY

To UNDERSTAND how herbalism fell under the influence of the stars, we need to look very briefly at the history of astrology. We shall then see why in so many of the older herbals a planet or zodiacal sign is attributed to each of the herbs listed, and why an authority like Culpeper can describe a given herb as curing any condition 'adversely influenced by Saturn in any part of the body governed by the Moon or Cancer, where the herb will cure by sympathy.'

The practice of astrology is believed to have originated in ancient Babylonia, where zealous priests first set about recording the behaviour of the heavenly spheres. Having noted that five visible planets existed besides our Sun and Moon, they related the movements of these to the major events of their time. The nature of such events then enabled these early astronomers to accredit the planets with certain general characteristics: thus to Ishtar, our Venus, were attributed the qualities of love and harmony, while their opposites, war and disruption, were the property of Nergal, our present-day Mars. Another important discovery of the same period was the celestial zodiac, a circular path along which the planets, the Sun and the Moon were then thought to travel.

Soon after its discovery, the zodiac was divided into twelve equal parts, each corresponding to a constellation along the ecliptic and each endowed with its own characteristics. In the meantime these new ideas were being carried along the trade routes to India whence they spread rapidly throughout the East.

19

Between 700 and 200 B.C. the mass of astronomical data gathered by the Babylonian priesthood continued to grow and the first horoscopes were cast. At the same time the starry wisdom spread to other Middle Eastern peoples, among them the Jews and Egyptians. The latter adapted the Babylonian system to their own needs, although there is evidence that astrology of a sort flourished in the kingdoms of the Nile long before then. There is evidence too of an astrological system remarkably like the systems of the Old World among the Aztec and Mayan civilizations in Central America. We can only speculate whether this was an isolated development or whether the people of both hemispheres had access to a common store of knowledge.

But it was above all the Greeks who turned astrology into the unified and, given its premises, logical system with which we are familiar. Although astrology was known to them from very early times, it was the invasion of Mesopotamia and subsequent contact with Babylon that stimulated fresh interest in the subject. Soon, its principles were assimilated by the major philosophical schools, the Stoics in particular laying stress on the influence of the stars on human affairs.

In ancient Rome astrology flourished as never before, despite the jibes of opponents like Cicero, Cato and Juvenal. This was still the position when Christianity, itself generally hostile to astrology, became the official religion of Rome. Even afterwards, astrological beliefs persisted among the Gnostics and neo-Platonists. Meanwhile, as the might of Rome fell into decline, so a new Arab civilization came into being in North Africa. There astrology was studied by the greatest scholars of the Muslim world and from there, in the twelfth century, it returned to Europe, much the richer for its exile.

By the time of the Renaissance, the popularity of astrology was more widespread in Europe than at any time before and the stars were now deemed to rule all human conduct. Then, suddenly, physicians discovered that the planets also have a part to play in the treatment of the sick. One of the first to develop this theory was Marsilio Ficino (1433–99) who, in his *Liber de Vita*, tells his readers which zodiacal signs rule different bodily parts and what effect the planets have on each of them. Paracelsus, whom we shall be meeting later, likewise strove to reconcile medicine with astrology, comparing the 'inner stars' of Man, the microcosm, to their stellar counterparts within the macrocosmic scheme.* On a more practical level this involved analysing the astrological significance of an illness, and prescribing for its treatment a substance whose astrological virtues suggested a possible cure. This was how mercury, once the only effective remedy for syphilis, first came to be prescribed for that condition. The reasoning here was that a 'mercurial' substance would alone curb the nefarious influence of the 'heavy' planets causing the disease.

Astrology remained successful regardless of the astronomical discoveries of stalwarts like Copernicus, Galileo and Kepler. Indeed, Kepler was for years a professional caster of horoscopes, though at times inclined to dismiss astrology as the foolish daughter of astronomy. Only in the eighteenth century, the Age of Enlightenment, did astrology finally lose favour, and not until two hundred years later did it start to regain it. By now, as everybody knows, astrology is as popular as it ever was.

The traditional defence of astrology is that our solar universe is part of a gigantic cosmic pattern whose characteristics are discernible from the position of the planets at any given moment. In other words, astrology depends on the assumed unity of the universe in which we live, a unity that postulates the interdependence of its constituent parts. This means that anything happening to one of these parts will to some extent affect the rest, the actual extent being determined by the closeness of their relationship. What astrologers have done, there-fore, is attempt to codify the relationship obtaining among various things within the universe, the occult connection, so to speak, between the planets and assorted scents, colours, precious stones and herbs. These connections, known as astrological correspondences, are of immense value to the occultist since they provide him with his key to the understanding of nature. For the occult-minded herbalist, they are, in addition, the means of knowing which plants to prescribe for different ailments.

Before we lose ourselves in esoteric theory, let me attempt to make things clearer by explaining how I learned the rudiments of astro-herbalism from my mentor, Mr James, Tan'rallt.

Herbs, he told me, conform, like everything else, with the general

* Paracelsus (see pp. 28–9) went as far as to state that astrological considerations govern even the administration of medicines: 'a medicine beneficial at one time can be harmful at another, depending on the planetary influence' (*Paramirum* III).

pattern we call nature. In their case each plant has been related to one of the twelve signs of the zodiac or brought under the influence of a particular planet. All this struck me as rather vague, until Mr James produced from his pocket a small fern-like plant. Its name I have since learned is adder's tongue (*Ophioglossum vulgare*), but all I learned from Mr James was that its celestial ruler is the Moon. The same planet, he explained, is also the ruler of Cancer, so that in this instance the herb falls within that sign. Now, the human body, like the rest of nature, can similarly be related to the signs of the zodiac, each of which governs a different bodily part or function. Cancer, for example, governs the breast and stomach so that, by sympathy, a Cancerian herb should relieve afflictions in those parts of the body. For that reason, adder's tongue was once prescribed in many cases of indigestion, where its antacid properties work to good effect. Likewise, pain and soreness in the breasts are often soothed by an ointment containing the same herb. This ointment, known as Charitable Oil, has long been a trusty reliever of all forms of inflammation and bruising.

On leaving Mr James I went straight home and set about learning which parts of my anatomy belonged to which signs of the zodiac. Here, for the benefit of readers inclined to compound their herbal nostrums on an astrological basis, is a table giving them the information they will need.

Sign	Ruling Planet	Part of body	Bodily system
Aries	Mars	Head	Cerebral
Taurus	Venus	Neck, throat	—
Gemini	Mercury	Hands, arms, lungs	Nervous
Cancer	Moon	Breast, stomach	Alimentary
Leo	Sun	Heart, spine, lower arm	Cardiac
Virgo	Mercury	Abdomen, hands, intestines	Visceral
Libra	Venus	Lower back, kidneys	Renal
Scorpio	Mars	Pelvis, sex organs	Generative
Sagittarius	Jupiter	Hips, thighs, liver	Hepatic

Sign	Ruling Planet	Part of body	Bodily system
Capricorn	Saturn	Knees, bones	—
Aquarius	Saturn	Shin, ankles	Circulatory
Pisces	Jupiter	Feet	Hepatic

In addition to knowing which parts of the body come under the dominion of each zodiacal sign, it is also necessary to know the planet whose special patronage each herb enjoys. This information can be gleaned from most older herbals, but for ease of reference the following table shows common herbs and their ruling planets. Further details concerning the medicinal use of these and other herbs may be found in the herbal *materia medica* in Chapter 9.

SUN
Burnet, camomile, celandine, centaury, chicory, eyebright, heartsease, marigold, mistletoe, pimpernel, rosemary, saffron, St John's wort, sundew, viper's bugloss.

MOON
Adder's tongue, chickweed, cleavers (goose-grass), loosestrife, privet, purslane, rose (white), watercress, white poppy, willow.

MERCURY
Dill, fennel, hazel, honeysuckle, lily-of-the-valley, maidenhair, marjoram, mulberry, parsley, southernwood, vervain.

VENUS
Alder, birch, blackberry, burdock, coltsfoot, cowslip, daisy, elder, fennel, foxglove, ground ivy, groundsel, marshmallow, meadowsweet, mint, mugwort, periwinkle, plantain, primrose, sanicle, sea holly, sorrel, tansy, thyme, valerian, vervain, violet, yarrow.

MARS
Basil, broom, hawthorn, lesser celandine, stonecrop, thistle, toadflax, wormwood.

JUPITER
Agrimony, balm, betony, borage, chervil, chestnut, cinquefoil, dandelion, dock, houseleek, hyssop, rose (red), sage, thistle.

SATURN
Bistort, comfrey, hemlock, henbane, ivy, knapweed, moss, mullein, nightshade.

From these tables it will be seen how simple it is, in theory at least, to find the usefulness of any herb, once its astrological significance has been ascertained. The exercise is further simplified because no less important than the zodiacal sign related to a plant's ruling planet is the occult significance of the planet itself. This again will often indicate the use to which nature intended a particular plant to be put. Let us, for example, take the lunar herbs, some of which, like adder's tongue, cure afflictions in the bodily parts ruled by Cancer. Others, however, being sacred to the Moon as Mistress of the Night, are soporifics and, like the red poppy (*Papaver rhoeas*), are frequently prescribed as such. In exactly the same way a solar herb like scarlet pimpernel will often act as a heat fortifier (Leo ruled by the Sun) and as a general tonic (the Sun), while a herb of Venus like periwinkle will soothe throat ulcers (Taurus ruled by Venus) and improve the complexion (Venus).

These, then, are some of the fundamentals of astrological herbalism. It should be mentioned too that the really dedicated follower of the system will check on planetary conditions even before he sets about harvesting his plants. By so doing he hopes to ensure that the planet linked with the herb he is gathering will not be ill placed in relation to its neighbours on the day in question. The theory is that if the planet were adversely positioned, the power of the herb would be sympathetically depleted. Personally, I find collecting herbs enough trouble without bothering at the same time about the arrangement of the heavens.

Earlier in this chapter we noted that astro-medicine came to the fore during the fifteenth century. It had existed before then, however, and both Hippocrates and Galen believed that every trainee physician should have a grounding in astronomy. Even so, astrological medicine was first systemized during the Renaissance, yielding some years later the earliest astrological herbals. In these the rulership of a sign or planet is bestowed on all the plants of forest, field and hedgerow. Among such herbals were those of Carrichter and Propp in Germany and, in England, the *Botanologia* of Robert Turner. Another astrological herbalist was Nicholas Culpeper, whose fame survives to this day.

Culpeper, the son of a parson, was born in 1616. He showed an early interest in science and astrology, and, as a young man, studied medicine at the University of Cambridge. During the Civil War he became a committed Parliamentarian, fighting on behalf of that cause until a serious chest wound put him out of action. Its effects were never to leave him and he suffered from tuberculosis for the remainder of his life. With his medical training and knowledge of the planets he set himself up as a herbalist and astrologer in Red Lion Street, Spital-fields, where he soon attracted a large number of patients. Among them were many poor people whom he treated for nothing, a kindness that earned him a philanthropic reputation but kept him in penury for most of his days. By all accounts his cures were astounding, much to the dismay of the College of Physicians, which responded by attacking him in sundry pamphlets and papers. Culpeper died at the early age of thirty-eight, but in his last years he had sought to make known his methods of treatment by publishing books on the medicinal use of herbs. These, consolidated in the famous *Culpeper Herbals*, are still read today, and the headquarters of the Society of Herbalists in London is named Culpeper House in his honour.

Despite their fondness for Culpeper, contemporary herbalists tend to be embarrassed by the erstwhile marriage between herbalism and astrology. Some would like to pretend that it never took place. And yet many of the plants used now by both herbalists and modern pharmacology owe their discovery to that strange celestial science which began in Babylon a long long time ago.

It may be, of course, that some plants acquired their astrological trappings *after* their therapeutic worth had been confirmed through trial and error, but the true sequence of events, like the chicken and the egg, is now too remote for us to determine. What is certain is that no student of herbalism, however sceptical, can ignore its astro-logical connections. The same is true of yet another herbalist curiosity, the so-called Doctrine of Signatures, the subject of our next chapter.

The zodiacal influences on the body

3
THE DOCTRINE OF
SIGNATURES

ASTROLOGY IS not the only 'occult' explanation foisted on herbalism. Equally important is the Doctrine of Signatures, according to which the appearance of certain herbs provides a clue to their use in medicine.

Where this doctrine came from nobody can tell, but there are grounds for thinking it was prevalent throughout the ancient world. In the West it belongs to a mystical tradition that flourished in Alexandria which, from its foundation in 331 B.C., was the home of alchemy and magic. Here scientists like Ostanes the Mede, Synesius and Maria Prophetissa pursued the great secret that would transmute base metal into gold. In their search they were led by the conviction that all things are formed of a common substance, the *prima materia*, differences among them being due to the presence of varying elementary qualities. By removing these qualities the alchemist tried to create for himself this primary matter or 'celestial mercury', as it was sometimes called. From there his next step was to restore to it the qualities of whatever substance he wished to reproduce in his laboratory. Thus by adding to primary matter the characteristic qualities of gold, an alchemist might end up with the real eighteen-carat stuff.

Implicit in the Doctrine of Signatures is a similar belief in the essential oneness of nature. (It is, as we have observed, a belief common to astrology as well.) What proponents of the Doctrine insist, however, is that Man, the microcosm, enjoys a privileged relationship with the outside world, the macrocosm, of which he is a tiny copy. Between Man and nature, therefore, there is held to exist a subtle connection arising from their fundamental oneness. It follows, then, that the appearance of the natural world about us, its plants, flowers, trees and stones, display this connection to anyone who has the eyes to see its presence.

What we are asked to believe, in short, is that nature is full of meaning, its external aspect bearing always the mark of its inner significance. As far as the herbalist is concerned, this means that the healing virtues of various plants can be discerned from their appearance – from, that is, the peculiar 'signature' they bear.

How does this work in practice?

The question is best answered by a few examples. Among these we have the lesser celandine, a familiar hedgerow plant which, as you will discover if you pull it up, sprouts tiny nodules from its root. Here, says the Doctrine of Signatures, is proof positive of its value as a cure for haemorrhoids. By the same token, the wild pansy with its heart-shaped leaves is seen as a potent cardiac tonic. Likewise, plants whose leaves are kidney-shaped are adjudged good for the renal system, while spotted leaves are assumed to cure acne.

Sometimes, the connection between a plant and the malady it cures is not as evident as these few examples may suggest. While it is understandable why flame-coloured flowers should be thought to soothe inflammation, it is less easy, without a knowledge of colour symbolism, to understand why multi-coloured flowers were once deemed to stimulate the brain, or purple ones to be a tonic for the spleen.

Foremost among the defenders of the Doctrine of Signatures was Philipp Theophrastus Bombastus von Hohenheim, better known as Paracelsus,* who is often referred to as the first 'modern' scientist. Paracelsus, born in 1493, received an orthodox medical training at the University of Basle and, after a period as an army surgeon, returned there in 1526 to take up the chair of medicine. At his inaugural lecture he began by burning Avicenna's *Canon of Medicine*, one of the most respected medical works of the time. This gesture, and the novelty of his theories and treatments, earned him the unremitting hostility of his colleagues, who in 1528 forced him to give up his post

---

* According to Paracelsus, we recognize the signatures instinctively: 'The mind need not concern itself with the physical constitution of plants and roots. It recognizes their powers and virtues intuitively thanks to the signatures they carry' (*De natura rerum*).

and quit the city. From then on until his death in 1541 he wandered around Europe, writing, curing the sick and seeking at every turn to increase his knowledge of medicine. 'The universities', he declared, 'do not teach us everything; a good physician should be ready to learn from midwives, gipsies, nomads, brigands and others who live outside the law. He should inquire among all classes of people, seeking out everything that might contribute to his knowledge; he should travel widely, undergo many adventures and learn, learn all the while.'*

Occult subjects were among those studied by Paracelsus during his lifetime, and here it was his privilege to be taught by such eminent scholars as the alchemist Salomon Trismosin, the sorcerer Trithemius (see p. 39) and, possibly, by Agrippa, the greatest magus of that period. In accordance with hermetic tradition Paracelsus was convinced that human life was mysteriously bound up with that of the universe. He believed too that the clay from which Man had been created contained all existing chemicals, but predominant among them were sulphur, salt and mercury. Sickness, he maintained, followed whenever there occurred a deficiency of one or more of these three vital chemicals, but in a healthy person all coexisted in just the right proportions, bound together by a subtle fluid called the 'archaeus' whose source lay in the stomach.†

The same chemicals were also present, in varying quantities, throughout the vegetable world. Thus by taking the appropriate herb, a sick person could ingest whatever chemicals his constitution lacked. In this way he would be restored to health. The great doctor further taught, as Aristotle had before him, that plants (characterized, like the humours, as hot, cold, moist and dry) contained a therapeutic principle, not unlike the archaeus, from which patients taking herbal medicines could benefit.

For the most complete exposition of the Doctrine of Signatures we must turn to a fascinating Neapolitan called Giambattista della Porta. Della Porta (1543–1615) was a scientist, alchemist, magician and gentleman-farmer. It was this last occupation that stimulated his interest in herbs, and during his lifetime he published two works on

* *Defensiones*, Liber iv.

† 'The archaeus is the power that gives everything its nature, distinguishing one thing from another and giving each its "seed" [*semen*].' *Liber Meteorum*.

29

the subject, the *Phytognomonica* and *Villa*, the latter a description of various plants, their fanciful origins, and their cultivation and value to mankind. His devotion to the Doctrine of Signatures led him to search for signs of a plant's medicinal value not only in the form of its leaves and petals but in minute dissections of its every part. He also studied a plant's behaviour, its flowering season and its methods of propagation. According to him, too, the places where various plants were wont to grow offered precious information to the perspicacious herbalist. He even asserted that plants common to a particular region would cure the afflictions of its inhabitants, the theory being that the local climate was responsible both for diseases and their cure.

These ideas aroused some controversy, but on the whole herbalists of the period, especially those with pious or mystical inclinations, tended to accept them. The English herbalist Robert Turner was a

WILLOW

stout defender of the Doctrine in his *Botanologia*. But with the arrival of the eighteenth century and the subsequent growth of experimental medicine, the need for 'doctrines' of this sort gradually disappeared. Instead, science adopted the more pragmatic approach which we know today. Herbalism, too, slowly shed its dependence on astrology and 'signatures', preferring instead to judge a plant by the results it gave and not by the shape of its stamen or the bumps on its root.

And yet, to be fair to the shades of Paracelsus and della Porta, we cannot dismiss the Doctrine of Signatures quite so flippantly. It is an inescapable fact that many of the herbal remedies still prescribed were first discovered because someone took the trouble to read the botanical signature believed to have been left by a providential nature. Our friend the lesser celandine does, after all, cure haemorrhoids, although whether this is because of or despite the pile-like nodules on its root is anybody's guess. And the wild pansy, blessed with tiny heart-shaped leaves, really does cure valvular disorders of the heart. There are many more examples to be found, but those readers who are interested can find them for themselves. While doing so, they may care to note that even della Porta's extension of the Doctrine to the actual site favoured by wild plants can be justified by a host of examples. Take the willow tree, for instance, which because it grows in damp places was assumed to provide a cure for rheumatism, a condition aggravated, if not caused, by a damp atmosphere. In accordance with the Doctrine, willow bark was duly prescribed for the easing of rheumatic pain, and, curiously, it worked. But still more curious is that when modern science deigned to take an interest in the willow, it discovered a substance to which it gave the name of salicin (Latin *salix*=willow), once an important stand-by in the treatment of rheumatic fever. The same substance plays its part too in the history of aspirin (acetysalicylic acid), undoubtedly one of the safest and most efficient painkillers yet discovered.*

By now the Doctrine of Signatures is an historical curiosity, but we all have reason to feel glad it had its day.

* It should be noted that the glucoside salicin ($C_{13}H_{18}O_7$) is found in other plants besides the willow. As for salicylic acid (HOC_6H_4COOH), the progenitor of aspirin, that too is found in many herbs, e.g. those of the *spiraea* group. It is also present in birch bark (see p. 87) and, abundantly, in wintergreen (*Gaultheria procumbens*), a plant long used in the botanical treatment of rheumatism.

St John's wort

4

THE PREPARATION
OF HERBS

MOST HERBS can be bought ready dried from any herbalist supplier, and the commoner varieties are also found on sale in health food shops. The cheapest way of obtaining herbs, however – and the most satisfying – is to pick them for yourself. Although the task is made much easier if you live out in the country or have access to it, there is no cause for despair should your existence be an urban one. The fact is that some of our most virtuous herbs grow unnoticed in back gardens and on grimy city wastes. Indeed, it may surprise you, when you read the list of plants given in Chapter 9, to see the number of familiar weeds included there. These are available to all.*

The best time for gathering herbs is on a sunny morning in spring or early summer, preferably just after the dew has evaporated from them. Care should always be taken to avoid picking wet plants as these are liable to turn mouldy. Once gathered, your herbs must be dried, unless, of course, they are required for immediate use. Generally speaking, herbs gathered when the moon is waning dry the quickest since they then have far less sap in their leaves and stems. On the other hand, if the root is wanted, that is best unearthed when the moon is waxing, since then all roots are at their tenderest. In the case of certain herbs, the flowers are the part employed in medicine and so their harvesting has naturally to coincide with the flowering season of the plant.

* But do make sure, before you gather these and any other plants, that they have not been doused in weed-killer or other toxic liquids. Be wary, too, of plants that grow along busy roadsides where they are bombarded with car exhausts.

The actual drying of herbs is no great problem. The best way of going about it is to hang them up in bunches in a well-ventilated room. (When roots are being dried, it is often a good idea to cut them lengthwise before you start.) In cold climates or in damp weather the natural drying process may have to be supplemented by a little artificial heat: all I do at such times is leave my herbs in front of the fire for an hour or so each day. They can, however, be oven-dried, care being taken not to let the temperature rise above 35°C (94°F); anything higher may affect the volatile oils and other active principles in the plant. For the same reason sunlight is unsuitable for drying most herbs, the aromatics in particular, and as a general rule drying should take place in the shade. Once dried, the herbs should be broken into fragments and stored in jars, paper bags or tins. They will then keep for about three years.

Next we come to the preparation of herbs for use. Infusions, the commonest method of taking herbal medicine, are prepared by pouring a pint of boiling water over an ounce of dried herb (three handfuls of the fresh) and leaving the mixture for three to four hours. (Large leaves should be cut first, and tough herbs finely chopped.) Some herbalists prefer to add cold water to the herb, which is then heated gently in a saucepan until boiling point is reached. The liquid is left to simmer for no more than two minutes before being removed from the heat and allowed to brew for a further three hours. Infusions like these, referred to later in the text as 'standard', will keep fresh for up to four days (slightly longer if intended for external use) if poured into bottles and stored in a cool dark place. Instead of corking the bottles, put some muslin or perforated greaseproof paper over their tops.

When an infusion of this sort is prepared for immediate use, being allowed to brew for no longer than a cup of tea, it is called a tisane. You will find this word used again later in the text. Because tisanes brew for so short a time, it is advisable to use more herb in their case – say, one teaspoonful of dried herb (three of fresh) per cup. The same is true of herbal teas.

Sometimes herbs – and especially their roots – are used in the form of a decoction. To make this, simmer half an ounce of dried root in one pint of water for as long as it takes – usually some twenty minutes – to reduce the water to half a pint. Afterwards the root, by then soft and tender, can be strained off and the liquid stored in exactly the same way as before. In general, decoctions tend to stay fresh longer than other herbal brews.

As for herbal creams and ointments, there are two ways of preparing these. The first is to cook one ounce of finely crushed herb in three-quarters of a pound of lard until the herb is well and truly incorporated in the fat. Before it cools, strain the fat into a suitable container and leave it to set. To harden the final ointment, add some beeswax to the strained fat, reheat gently and allow the mixture to cool. The second method is the more violent, since it involves pounding one part of fresh or dried herbs into two parts of bland cold cream. A mortar and pestle should enable you to manage this without great hardship.

There remain a few other methods of using herbs. One is the herbal tincture which takes about three weeks to produce and requires three ounces of powdered herb to a quart of surgical spirit. The tincture is stored in an airtight jar or bottle that must be kept in a warm place and given a vigorous shake every other day.

Essential oils are only a shade more trouble to prepare. In their case two tablespoonfuls of finely crushed herb are put in a half-pint bottle which is thereupon three-quarters filled with pure vegetable oil. Add to this a tablespoonful of plain (not malt) vinegar, cork the bottle and store in a warm place, ideally in hot sunlight. Essential oils require about three weeks to mature, by which time they should hold the scent of whatever herbs they happen to contain. To make an extra strong preparation, strain off the oil at the end of the first and second weeks and each time introduce it to a fresh quantity of herbs. In cold weather the whole process can be helped along by placing the bottle in warm water for an hour or so each day.*

Herbal poultices, whose virtue lies in their ability to draw poisons from the body, can be prepared in a variety of ways. Easiest of all perhaps is to apply hot macerated herb to the part due for treatment, keeping it there by means of a tight bandage or plaster. A more traditional poultice can be had by preparing a standard infusion and adding to it cornflour or powdered slippery elm until a thin paste is obtained. Spread this paste on a clean linen bandage and apply to the affected part. Useful poultice herbs are comfrey, poppy, violet, St John's wort

---

* Some herbalists go one step further and add the essential oil thus obtained to the appropriate quantity of alcohol (2 oz. of oil to 1 quart alcohol).

and adder's tongue. These and several others are listed in Chapter 9.

Finally, a word should be said about the quantities given in most herbal recipes. Frequently, when describing the ingredients of a particular nostrum, herbalists will refer loosely to amounts like a 'handful' or a 'pinch'. Similarly, the dosage – if given at all – is often expressed in vague terms like a 'cupful' or a 'wineglassful' to be taken 'up to three times daily'. This may worry cautious readers, given that nowadays the instructions on our medicines tend to be specific and to stress the dangers of going beyond the stated dose. But fortunately herbs, being less concentrated than most modern drugs, allow a certain latitude both in their preparation and their consumption. Where no specific dose is recommended, take two to three wineglassfuls (infusions) or one cupful (decoctions) daily. You will probably find that a pint of liquid fills a wineglass six times. In the following pages you will find that exact amounts are stated whenever the herb under consideration might do harm if taken to excess. Apart from such cases, there is no need to worry unduly about precise measures when following the many herbal remedies you will find described.

5

TONICS AND PHYSICS

THE WORD 'tonic' is not one that is approved by modern medicine. Nowadays, when patients say they feel run down, young doctors are advised to seek the causes of this feeling and to treat it as the symptom of a more specific illness. The advice is sound: the tiredness character-istic of anaemia, for example, can be treated with an iron-enriched tonic, but little benefit ensues if the intestinal bleeding that may be causing the anaemia is left to go unchecked. For that reason any reader who feels perpetually tired, listless and depressed might do well to see his doctor before embarking on a herbal cure.

I emphasize 'perpetually' tired, listless and depressed, because many of us feel that way from time to time. On such occasions there is probably no grave disorder troubling us, and our general malaise is simply caused by the wear and tear of living. It is at times like these that herbal tonics come in useful.

These tonics work in several ways, depending on the herbs included in them. Some of their ingredients are nutritional supplements, mostly rich in vitamins and essential minerals. As such they differ little from their more synthetic rivals found on sale in chemists' shops. It should be noted, however, that supplements of this sort, natural or synthetic, are quite unnecessary when a normal diet is being followed. Their usefulness arises because under stress or illness the appetite may suffer and so reduce the vitamin intake just when the need for extra vitamins is at its greatest.

The effect of other tonic herbs springs from their chemical con-stituents, most of which stimulate beneficial responses in our bodies.

(Many are plants that contain alkaloids widely used and copied in modern pharmacology.) The work they do may vary from a simple thing like perking up the appetite to a diathetic change of the subtlest kind. Thanks to these the tired organism is restored to peak condition.

Other herbs do not appear to work directly on the body, but affect instead the brain and nervous centres.* The exact process is unknown, but one theory is that they affect the biochemistry that constitutes our thinking. In this way they inspire a new sense of well-being – just as certain drugs induce euphoria – and persuade the body – psychosomatically – to improve itself.

But for our present purposes there is little point in speculating how these herbs work, provided the results obtained from them are satisfactory. Having said that, let me admit that one or two of the tonic recipes shown below are rather suspect in the eyes of modern herbalists since their compilation has depended on the astrological significance of the plants employed. Even so, many of these plants are well respected for their medicinal worth, regardless of the astral connotations, so it would be wrong to dismiss them out of hand.

DIOD ANFARWOLDEB

Literally, the 'draught of immortality', this recipe contains some of nature's most potent herbs, providing a general tonic of immense value. I came across this recipe in the centre of Anglesey, and was assured it was the invention of the Druids who formerly inhabited that island! Certainly it is very ancient, and two of its ingredients, vervain and clover, were among the seven sacred herbs of the early Celtic priesthood.

Prepare a standard infusion from the following herbs: chervil, heather, honeysuckle, red clover and vervain. Take a tablespoonful night and morning as long as you need a tonic.

AURUM POTABILE PARACELSI

Solar gold to revitalize the whole system is what this happy conjunction of sun-ruled herbs is intended to provide. They consist of marigold, rosemary and sundew. Their effect is much enhanced by the

---

*Dr Edward Bach was one of the first to study the way in which certain herbs, by their effect on the mind, are able to cure physical diseases, especially those whose origin is psychosomatic. See N. Weeks, *The Medical Discoveries of Dr Edward Bach, Physician* (Rochester, C. W. Daniel, 1940).

addition of rock-rose (*Helianthemum nummularium*),* a plant noted for its anti-depressant qualities. The mixture suits all age groups, including young infants, and a cupful of the standard infusion should be taken on rising.

AQUA MIRABILIS

A seventeenth-century panacea which once enjoyed tremendous success; its ingredients comprise cinnamon, galingale root, ginger, thyme, rosemary and grated nutmeg. These should all be finely ground and steeped in claret for a week, after which the wine is strained and a glassful taken daily.

This concoction was alleged to restore vigour, refresh the spirit and bring warmth and comfort in old age. The claret doubtless played its part in all of this.

CELESTIAL POTION

Lily-of-the-valley, loosestrife, marjoram (*Origanum vulgare*) and vervain, these lunar and mercurial herbs, each with specific rejuvenating properties, make up this potion. All are known for their ability to conserve youth and physical fitness and, as such, are ideal for people past the age of forty. A cupful of standard infusion should be taken daily.

To cure depression, add a pinch of woodruff (*Galium odoratum*) and for the special benefit of elderly patients substitute some Iceland moss (*Cetraria islandica*) for any one of the plants already listed.

ELIXIR VITAE

Calomel, gentian, cinnamon, aniseed, nard and mace – these are the ingredients of a potion devised by the arch-mage Trithemius (1462–1516), who began life as a beggar boy and ended it as Abbot of Spanheim, near Würzburg. Trithemius was profoundly interested in alchemy and magic, but despite his occult prowess *and* the vital elixir, he died at the age of fifty-four.

Five grammes of the mixture should be taken daily in wine. To the ingredients recommended by Trithemius add, if you wish, some marsh pennywort (*Hydrocotyle vulgaris*), a plant said to promote healthful longevity.

Rejuvenating medicines like the elixir of Abbot Trithemius are a

* A plant's botanical name will be given only when that plant does not appear among those described in Chapter 9.

common feature of herbal literature. It is important to remember that in this context the word 'rejuvenating' is often a synonym for aphrodisiac. Thus when old herbals speak of restoring a patient's lost youth, what they have in mind is the fire in his loins not the smoothness of his cheeks.

In selecting the plants by which the elderly or faint-hearted might improve their sexual prowess, early herbalists relied heavily on the Doctrine of Signatures. Thus the mandrake, its forked root not unlike our own lower parts, became an early champion of the cause of Venus. Associated with it, appropriately enough, was the superstition that it grew only at crossroads where there stood a gibbet, and where it could be nourished with the semen of hanged men. Such was the plant's sinister reputation that its harvesting became a very tricky business. The usual method involved tethering a dog to the plant and enticing him away with a piece of meat. The hope was that the dog would pull up the root and bring upon himself the mandrake's wrath. Such precautions were deemed necessary because rumour had it that mandrakes harmed anyone who dared uproot them. Sometimes an abused mandrake would shriek with such fury that it deafened or drove to madness whoever heard it – which is why the prudent herbalist stayed out of earshot while his dog did the dirty work for him.*
It is likely that these stories were invented by itinerant doctors, many of whom made a good profit selling mandrakes and were naturally fearful lest people start gathering their own. Contemporary rejuvenators need therefore fear no supernatural mishaps when out in search of mandrakes.

The pharmacological uses of the mandrake will be looked at in the next chapter, but we can ask ourselves here whether there are any grounds for the belief in its aphrodisiac virtues. Apart from its magical connections, mandrake root contains an alkaloid called mandragorine which, like the atropine in belladonna (deadly nightshade), can affect the mind, inducing anything from exaltation to complete sedation. It is possible, therefore, that small doses of the plant have in the past helped nervous lovers shed their inhibitions, thus making their performance that much better. To that extent it works.

* Shakespeare refers to this belief in *Romeo and Juliet* where the heroine says:
'And shrieks like mandrakes torn out of the earth;
That living mortals, hearing them, run mad.'

Historically the orchid vies in importance with the mandrake as an aphrodisiac. Again the Doctrine of Signatures may have influenced herbalists who saw orchid creepers intertwined with trees and compared this with the act of sexual congress. In other types of orchid the signature may well lie in their root tubers which, to the biased eye, resemble the shape of testes, the word orchid itself being derived from the Greek word for testicle.

Throughout the Middle Ages herbals gave advice on how to produce a rejuvenating potion from the stately purple orchid (*Orchis mascula*). Taken in small doses twice daily, such a draught, we are informed, 'causeth great heat; therefore it giveth lust unto the workes of generacyon and multiplycation of spermes'.* So widely esteemed were the orchid's powers as a sexual restorative that by the seventeenth century a powder – salep – made from its dried tubers was the basis of a popular beverage. At one stage it even rivalled coffee, and a salep house flourished for a time in Fleet Street.

It is not clear why the use of salep fell out of favour, unless its taste and texture in solution made it unattractive. (I am told it was often mixed with wine, which may well have been to render it more palatable.) Possibly, too, it was found that it did nothing for the libido.†

Whether other herbal aphrodisiacs were any more effective it is difficult to say. Among them were the sweet potato (*Convolvulus batatas*) and sea holly whose candied roots were a favourite Elizabethan comfit. I remember hearing once that sea holly was also added to the corn of stud horses to build up their resources but I have never come across its aphrodisiac use outside the stable. Another prized rejuvenant was the rocket flower (*Hesperis matronalis*)‡ and in his *Physician's Guide to Plants* Culpeper draws attention to its sperm-producing qualities. These, incidentally, were being recommended as late as

---

* From Hieronymus Brunselwig's *Liber de ante distillandi* (1527), as translated by Laurence Andrew.

† The orchid's reputation as a rejuvenator is, however, not completely lost. A famous French cosmetic firm still produces creams containing its pollen.

‡ It must be recorded that authorities disagree over the identity of the aphrodisiac variety of rocket. Above I have proposed dame's violet (*Hesperis matronalis*) as the rightful candidate, but others opt for creeping yellow cress (*Rorippa sylvestris*) or even common yellow rocket (*Barbarea vulgaris*). Less controversial is damiana (*Turnera aphrodisiaca*), a Central American native obtainable from most herbalists.

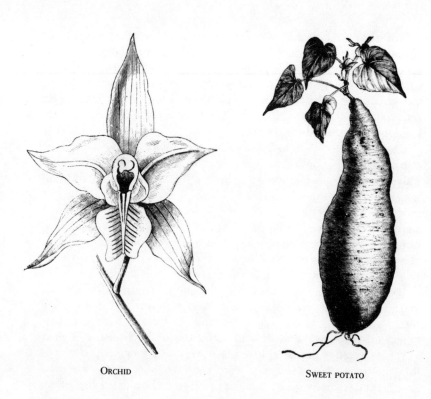

ORCHID

SWEET POTATO

1952 in a book aptly entitled *Venus in the Kitchen**: Plants with the appropriate magical associations were naturally strong contenders for recognition as potential aphrodisiacs, especially those plants whose astrological connection was with Venus. Fennel and vervain are just two examples of these. Rather more sophisticated is the use by one herbalist I know of blackberry leaves to cure impotence when its cause is psychological. The reasoning here is that as the blackberry is governed by Venus, planet of love, in the sign of Aries, ruler of the head, it will banish sexual inhibitions. My friend assures me that it never fails.†

* B. Pilaff and D. Norman, London, Heinemann, 1952.

† For the sake of completeness I should perhaps mention that *excessive* ardour can be cooled with infusions of strawberry leaf.

Not all herbal tonics are concerned with rejuvenation, whether sexual or not. Let us look, therefore, at a few others and note any special properties they have.

TONIQUE D'AVICENNE

In this recipe, herbs to prevent hardening of the arteries and other adverse vascular conditions collaborate with known heart fortifiers to provide a sovereign cardiac tonic. They are: mistletoe, rue, heartsease and rosemary (or vervain as an alternative).

Prepare a standard infusion and take a sherry-glassful before breakfast. Patients recovering from heart attacks will also benefit from the addition of pheasant's eye (*Adonis annua*).

This recipe is named after Husain Ibn 'Abd Allah (Ibn Sina), better known as Avicenna (980–1037), whose work – though, as we have seen, despised by Paracelsus – was studied in medical schools well into the seventeenth century. Avicenna wrote about heart drugs, but that scarcely explains why certain French herbalists attribute this tonic to him.

HIPPOCRATIC KIDNEY TONIC

eyebright	*nettle* or *parsley*
fennel	*violet*
groundsel or *meadowsweet*	

Despite its name, the only apparent link between this recipe and Hippocrates is that most of the herbs listed are among the four hundred simples known to have been used by him. Certainly, they all make up a fine kidney tonic whose diuretic virtues are well matched by its strong dissolvent properties. It can thus be used with confidence in the treatment of many kidney and bladder complaints. Make a standard infusion and take two tablespoonfuls daily.

NERVE NOSTRUM

balm or *lily-of-the-valley*	*skullcap*
lavender or *periwinkle*	*valerian*

Led by valerian and skullcap, this little army of nerve herbs has been marshalled to conquer all forms of nervous debility. Also worth putting in its ranks is balm, which quickly drives away depression. Take two tablespoonfuls of a standard infusion.

With these last three preparations we have moved from general tonics to nostrums for more specific ends. The fact is that herbs exist to cure most diseases that flesh is heir to, and a comprehensive *materia medica* is provided in the final chapter. From this the herb best suited to any given condition may be identified without difficulty. There are certain conditions, however, which are commoner than others and, here, several herbs may compete for inclusion in the treatment. To make things easier for the novice herbalist, a few simple nostrums are described below. Wise readers will take note of these and have their herbs gathered, mixed and ready-dried for the day when they are needed.

PHYSIG CRYD CYMALAU

candytuft or *meadowsweet*   *cowslip* or *rue*
cleavers   *nettle*
comfrey

A concentration of anti-arthritic and analgesic herbs makes this an efficient treatment of rheumatic and allied complaints. It is based on a Welsh recipe of considerable antiquity, one version of which offers seakale as a substitute for cleavers.

An infusion of the leaves should be made and a cupful taken daily. The treatment may be supplemented by the application of an ointment based on as many as possible of the same herbs.

Readers suffering from rheumatism should eat plenty of water-cress and celery. They may also care to note that gipsies in the Camargue often relieve rheumatic pain by stinging the affected spot with nettles. If vinegar is then rubbed over it, this dulls the sting but leaves behind a pleasing analgesic warmth. Much the same effect can be obtained from a poultice of ragwort (*Senecio jacobaea*).

SLEEPSOUND MIXTURE

A gentle non-addictive soporific composed of primrose or cowslip leaves (equal quantities), a few flowering sprigs of heather and just a dash of wild lettuce (*Lactuca virosa*). The primroses or cowslips may be used on their own, but go easy on the wild lettuce which is stronger stuff. The heather is nervine and has a tranquillizing effect. Half a cupful of the standard infusion should be taken one hour before going to bed.

To complete the treatment try sleeping on a pillow stuffed with dried hops or, better still, a traditional West Country mixture of lavender, peppermint, sage and dill. These last herbs will bring you none but the sweetest of dreams. Further details on soporific herbs will be found in the next chapter.

HERBS FOR HIGH BLOOD PRESSURE

Prepare a standard infusion using wallflower, primrose and sorrel (leaves of the last two, flowers – especially the yellow ones – of the first). One tablespoonful of this infusion, taken twice daily, is a safe and effective way of reducing high blood pressure.

Blood pressure that is too low can be raised by an infusion of dandelion leaves and lady's mantle (*Alchemilla vulgaris*).

BARK AND BLOSSOM LINCTUS

lavender   *marigold petals*
white clover (Trifolium repens)   *beech* or *elder* (use the soft inner bark)

Based on an old Balkan recipe, this mixture contains herbs that are said to cleanse the system and purify the blood. It is often prescribed for the internal treatment of acne. Drink a cupful of the standard infusion on rising.

CHEST TREASURE

An original combination of herbs – agrimony, coltsfoot, briar rose and maidenhair – known to bring fast relief to people plagued by persistent coughing. Long-term benefits are afforded by the briar rose and maidenhair, both strong fortifiers of the heart and lungs.

Prepare a standard infusion, adding to it a little chopped garlic, unless the taste of garlic puts you off – in which case do without it.*

GRANNY'S COUGH CURE

coltsfoot   *ground ivy*
horehound   *elder flowers* – if available
marshmallow

With their peerless reputation for soothing irritated membranes of the chest and throat, these herbs should stop the most persistent cough. They have a tonic effect on the lungs. For troublesome croup or whooping cough include some mouse ear (*Hieracium pilosella*) in the mixture.

HERBS FOR INFERTILITY

Infertility can have many causes and it would be madness to pretend that herbs provide a magic remedy. The herbs listed below are those traditionally prescribed for this condition: whether or not they work

* *Dosage:* where not specified, follow the dosage recommended on p. 36.

will depend always on the cause and its susceptibility to herbal treatment. The herbs are chicory (*Cichorium intybus*), feverfew, motherwort (*Leonurus cardiaca*), nettle, raspberry leaf, red clover, skullcap and watercress. Use them separately or combine as many as possible. Prepare a standard infusion and drink a wineglassful morning and night.

The following are some of the other female disorders amenable to herbal treatment with details, in brackets, of the appropriate plants: menstrual irregularity (devil's bit scabious, flowers only); excessive menstruation (ground ivy); retained afterbirth (marshmallow or horsetail); vaginal inflammation (raspberry leaf or rosemary); general debility during and after pregnancy (thyme).

LAVENGRO SLIMMING HERBS*

A trio of useful herbs – dandelion, fennel and rosemary – reinforced by bladderwrack, a seaweed that reduces adipose tissue. (Found on most beaches, bladderwrack (*Fucus vesiculosus*) is a stringy dark brown weed with little oval sacs along its fronds.) Prepare a standard infusion, using the whole of these plants except their root, and drink a wineglassful daily.

French herbalists suggest you add some bladderwrack to the bath as well and pinch your fattier parts while soaking. If the pinching is done under water it should be painless and will redistribute fatty deposits (*céllulite*) in the vicinity. Be warned that no herb and no amount of pinching will make you slim unless you also watch your diet.

ZEPHYR MOUTHWASH

Lavender to sweeten and water dock (*Rumex hydrolapathum*) to soothe, both these herbs are essential to oral hygiene. (They even strengthen the gums and tighten up loose teeth!) Prepare a strong infusion and rinse the mouth thoroughly as often as possible.

In cases of gingivitis or other gum disorders, add sanicle to the mixture.

HERBAL LAXATIVES

Regular bowel action has ceased to be the fetish it once was, but there are still people like my aunt Nellie who nightly soaked fifteen senna pods in a cup of water which she drank the following morning.

* See also p. 55.

Less drastic, for those who feel they need a laxative, are the following herbs which may be used separately or in the combinations shown. (Standard infusion, one cupful nightly.)

1 cleavers (goose grass)
sage

3 redcurrant leaf (Ribes rubrum)
twitch

2 fennel shoots
yellow flag (Iris pseudoacorus)

Note: should these herbs be over-zealous on your behalf or should your stomach be upset for any other reason, the following herbs, in a standard infusion, will quickly put things right again – yarrow, shepherd's purse (*Capsella bursa-pastoris*), wormwood.

THE DIVINE CORDIAL

Our chapter on health-giving mixtures would not be complete without a description of this famous beverage. It takes a full year to prepare, having in it a selection of spring, summer and autumn flowers. Any herbalist sufficiently dedicated to produce it deserves health and strength a-plenty!

The procedure begins in March, when the following ingredients are beaten together in a stout mortar: two ounces each of acorns, betony, orris root, cypress, gentian and sweet scabious. To these are added an ounce of cinnamon, the same of yellow sandalwood, two drachms ($\frac{1}{4}$ oz.) of mace, seven juniper berries and some coriander seeds. When these again have been reduced to a fine powder, all the ingredients plus the peel of six oranges are poured into a stone jar containing a gallon of spirits of wine. Well shaken and tightly corked, this vessel is put away in a cool place for three to four weeks.

At the end of this period the first spring flowers, violets, bluebells and daffodils, are dropped into the liquid. As the year progresses, more flowers are added as and when they become available: wallflowers, jasmine, borage, thyme, broom, honeysuckle, lavender, elder, camomile, lily-of-the-valley, St John's wort, marjoram and viper's bugloss. With the last of these the infusion is allowed to stand for nine more days before being distilled to yield two quarts of aromatic spirit.

We are reliably informed that this precious liquid not only smells divinely but provides a medicine far better than the elixir of life once brewed by Paracelsus (see p. 83).

MANDRAKE, showing blossoms and fruits

6

COSMETICS AND
NARCOTICS

FOR THOSE in search of beauty or lost youth, herbs have always held a special fascination, and one that our modern cosmetic industry seems ever ready to exploit. For this reason the cosmetic use of herbs is a subject to be broached with common sense, a rare attribute in those intent on finding beauty. Each year millions spend small fortunes in pursuit of it, some on surgeons who, at a price, will stitch up double chins or de-bag eyes, others on prodigiously expensive creams whose application is alleged to banish wrinkles. And despite all this, everybody ages and nothing herbs can do will stop it.

Where certain herbs can help, perhaps, is in improving the faces we were born with and, where possible, delaying the more obvious marks of time. In other words, herbs will not *create* youth or beauty, but will enable us to make the most of what we have of either.

An early experimenter in the field of herbal cosmetics was the Greek physician Galen (*c.*130–*c.*200) who is accredited with the invention of cold cream. Galen it was who hit upon the idea of melting together six ounces of white wax and a pound of oil of roses and then – here is the important part – stirring into this mixture a cupful of water laced with spirit vinegar. Since Galen's time the oil of roses has been replaced by almond oil or even liquid paraffin, although the best substitute is sunflower oil which is particularly rich in vitamins A and D. Similarly, synthetic chemical preservative can now be used instead of alcohol or spirit vinegar, However, it is probably easier to purchase bland cold cream ready-made from any chemist's shop.

The importance in herbalism of commercial cold cream (or the

49

home-made sort, should you feel keen enough to make some) is that it provides a base for almost every type of skin food. (A base of hog's fat can be used instead, but this has a tendency to dilate the pores and its smell is far less sweet.) To the base are added the appropriate ingredients meant to nourish or revitalize the skin. A simple example is the so-called *Pommade de Ninon de Lenclos*, which was nothing more than cold cream combined with the raw juice of houseleek. Her devotion to this unguent is said to have kept the lovely Ninon (1620–1705) free from wrinkles until she reached her seventies.*

The ingredients added by the ancients to their creams and ointments included honey, myrrh, spikenard,† wallflower, geranium and narcissus. (Our modern lanolin was also known to them, being called *æspon* by the Greeks.) Much of our knowledge of the beauty preparations popular in classical times comes from Pliny and Ovid, the latter's poem *Medicamina Faciei Feminaeae* being devoted entirely to the subject and containing numerous recipes. For a clear skin Ovid recommends three pounds each of lentils and best Libyan barley ground together and mixed with ten eggs. Once the mixture has dried it is re-ground and further mixed with hartshorn and six narcissus bulbs, peeled and finely chopped. To it were added three ounces of gum arabic, the same of Tuscan wheat and twenty ounces of Hymettus honey, the resulting paste to be smeared on the face and left there overnight. Any woman disposed to use it would do well to sleep alone.

The following are three other beauty preparations which deserve to be mentioned because of the success they formerly enjoyed.

ELIZABETHAN POMATUM
To bestow a bloom on the skin, melt a pound of hog's fat and boil in

---

* Before her bath the same lady is reported to have poured into the water a quart solution comprising four ounces of bicarbonate of soda and double that amount of sea salt. This she followed with three quarts of milk in which had been stirred three pounds of honey. Apart from being a beauty treatment, this bath reputedly eliminates the post-natal stretch marks from which some new mothers suffer. (Here a pinch of alum in the water helps as well.)

† An oil in which this herb (*Valeriana jatamansi*) was steeped is thought to have been the precious ointment with which Mary Magdalene washed the feet of Christ.

it four ounces of fresh rose petals and the same of cowslip leaves. After fifteen minutes, strain and allow the fat to harden in a suitable receptacle.

Fresh elder flowers may be used in place of rose petals.

CRÈME ANTIQUE DE CATHAY

oil of sweet almonds　　　　　　*2 oz. neutral white soap*
3 oz. white honey　　　　　　*1 egg yolk*
1 marshmallow root (decocted)　*1 drachm essence of bitter almonds*
spermacetti or *white wax*

In the eighteenth century the ingredients listed here were used by ladies of the Court, all of whom sought a preparation both to whiten and improve the complexion. The quantities given are assumed ones, but we do know that the mixture was prepared in a bain-marie. Before the cream was applied, the face was often steamed by holding it over a bowl of boiling water in which was infused a handful of dried camomile flowers. After steaming, the face was vigorously scrubbed.

DAME TROT'S HONEY

2 lb. honey (clarified)　　　　*¼ pint rosemary infusion*
4 bryony roots (diced and decocted)

Named after Trotula, a woman doctor from Salerno, whose fame spread throughout Renaissance Europe, this mixture contains three antique beautifiers. All were boiled together until the rosemary infusion had evaporated, after which the mixture could be strained and stored for use.

White pond-lily leaves were sometimes used instead of bryony. The special attraction of the latter was that its root often resembles a tiny human form, a mandrake-like characteristic that was believed to endow the plant with magical properties.

Magic has played a part in several herbal beauty treatments, some of whose other ingredients are of the 'eye of newt, and toe of frog' variety. Happily, the two following preparations, though associated with witchcraft, are free from such horrors: their efficacy derives only from the herbs they contain – plus, perhaps, a residuum of magic!*

---

*Some readers will have met these two preparations in my book *Magic: An Occult Primer* (London, Jonathan Cape, 1972), pp. 250–51.

ISIS LOTION

Gently warm half a pint of buttermilk to which has been added a handful of elder flowers, marigold petals, geranium leaves and one chopped clove of garlic. The mixture should simmer for forty minutes before being removed from the heat and left for five hours. It must then be re-heated and an ounce of honey added to it.

ANTI-WRINKLE EMULSION

Follow the previous instructions using half quantities and substituting the following herbal ingredients:

camomile	*strawberry leaves* * or *elder flowers*
white pond-lily leaves	*teasel (Dipsacus fullonum)*

An infusion of these same herbs may be mixed with fuller's earth or clay powder (obtainable from a pharmacy) to provide a botanical face pack. Include some yarrow or marigold petals if the skin is inclined to be greasy, sage or horsetail if prone to open pores.

EGYPTIAN SKIN CONDITIONER

As far as I know, there is nothing particularly Egyptian about this preparation, but it has been suggested to me that it derives its name from the gipsies (known once as 'Egyptians') among whom it used to be popular.

Choose three or more of the following herbs – pansy, chickweed, cleavers, meadowsweet and scarlet pimpernel – and make a standard infusion. Rinse the face with this lotion and leave to dry naturally. The daily use of this lotion will greatly improve the texture of the skin, particularly when the complexion is prone to spots and other unbecoming blemishes.

For more direct action on skin eruptions, prepare a tincture from any of the herbs listed above and apply to the affected area with a piece of cotton wool. For further details on the treatment of a troubled skin, including severe conditions such as acne, eczema, erysipelas etc., see the *materia medica* provided later.

ANGEL WATER

An infusion of rosemary, sow thistle (*Sonchus oleraceus*) and white

---

* Strawberry juice is also held to benefit the skin. Enthusiasts suggest you smear it over your face before going to bed and wash it off in the morning with chervil water. Others recommend a strawberry paste made from fresh strawberries (4 oz.), gum tragacanth ($\frac{1}{8}$ oz.) and violet powder (1 oz.).

pond-lily leaves, alone or combined, provides a soothing lotion for sore, inflamed or angry skin. It is especially good for sunburn.

CLARIFYING DEW

An infusion of elder flowers, wood sorrel and daisy heads is a traditional way of removing freckles. It will also lighten a sallow skin.

WART CURE

From a score of alleged wart removers, here are the most reliable: greater celandine, poppy seed, houseleek. Apply the raw juice of one of these on the offending wart every night and morning. An ointment containing basil is also said to help.

From the skin let us move to the scalp, and look at a few traditional recipes to condition, refine and, in one case at least, to restore the hair.

HERBAL HAIR AND SCALP LOTION

Prepare, fresh each week, a standard infusion using camomile, nettle, parsley and rosemary. Massage the scalp with this daily. For dry, brittle hair, massage twice weekly with an essential oil of one or more of these herbs. Where dandruff is present substitute cleavers for any one of these ingredients. A pinch of rue added to the mixture will dispose of any nits in temporary occupation.

TONIC RINSE

After shampooing, give the hair a final rinse with an infusion of horsetail and sage. This will add lustre to the hair and enhance its natural colour.

BALDNESS CURE

I cannot guarantee that these herbs will actually persuade a bald pate to sprout luscious new hair, but tradition insists that they do. At any rate they may be worth a try.

Prepare an infusion of betony, maidenhair fern and scarlet pimpernel. Massage well into the scalp once a day. An essential oil of yellow archangel (*Lamiastrum galeobdolon*) can be used to supplement the treatment.

HAIR COLOURANT

To impart a hint of chestnut to the hair, rinse it in an infusion of mature privet leaves and, if possible, allow it to dry in the sun. The Venetian beauties painted by Titian are known to have used this method to obtain their distinctive hair colouring. For a lighter, more golden shade, add quince juice, itself a good hair tonic, to the same infusion. Hair that is already fair may be lightened by rinsing with an infusion of camomile flowers.

In the Middle East there is a tradition that the peel of several green oranges steeped in oil for two to three months provides a lotion that will restore the colour to faded, grey or whitened hair. Hair can also be darkened by regularly washing it with an infusion of rosemary and red sage.

After face-washes and hair-rinses we come now to full-scale bathing, regarded as something of a beauty ritual since the very earliest times. The Romans caught the habit from the Greeks, but far excelled them in the splendour of their public baths. Here they gossiped, rubbed themselves with costly oils and soaked for hours in the scented water. The more enthusiastic bathers felt that water was not good enough, and copied Cleopatra with her famous bath of asses' milk. Others partial to more than just a common bath have been Mary Queen of Scots, who liked to bathe in claret, and the Countess Bathory, a Transylvanian lady who wallowed in the blood of virgins slaughtered in her castle cellar.

Less *recherché* is the tonic bath described by Ovid, which requires only lupin flowers scattered on the water. Sprigs of rosemary are also beneficial, being said to smooth the skin. In the East baths were often scented with aromatic herbs, and their beautifying possibilities increased by adding to them a jugful of rice and barley boiled in water. Sea salt and seaweed were also favourite additives, both being rich in iodine.

Readers wishing to emulate the ancients or simply to enhance the joys of bathtime may care to note the following recipes.

BEDYDD CERIDWEN

Literally 'Ceridwen's Baptism', a name inspired by the magic cauldron of Ceridwen which is described in the *Mabinogion*. There is an old Welsh tradition that the dedicated bather should spit three times before stepping into this bath which, despite its romantic name, consists only of elder leaves or cowslip flowers and a few sweet scabious sprinkled on the water.

A BEAUTY BATH

Here is a bath to add sheen to the skin and smooth dry patches on elbows, heels, etc. Prepare an essential oil of marigolds (petals only) and hyssop,* and add a tablespoonful to the water in your tub.

For more intimate douches it is doubtful whether a diluted infusion of oak leaves or white pond-lily leaves can ever be excelled.

A SLIMMING BATH

For a pleasing silhouette, add an infusion of dandelion, horsetail and rosemary to your bath water.

I must confess that I can see no reason why a bath like this should make you slim. But I do know that many herbalists prescribe these herbs and others (fennel, kale, etc.) when treating obesity. (Most of these herbs are mildly aperient.)

When the problem is to *gain* rather than lose weight, herbs like fenugreek (*Trigonella ornithopodioides*), camomile and royal fern (*Osmunda regalis*) are often recommended. (Standard infusions and one wineglassful daily.)

Finally, a nice warm bath before going to bed will give you all the beauty sleep you need. To be absolutely sure of that, sprinkle some valerian (leaves and diced root) or, if you have some, a generous pinch of henbane (*Hyoscyamus niger*) in the water.† With this last herb, however, we have already moved from cosmetic plants to those more sinister ones endowed with narcotic or, at least, soporific properties.

Herbal narcotics have been used since primitive times. Our ancestors prized them highly because they dulled the senses and so negated pain. In addition, they were a means of self-intoxication by which the mind achieved communion with the supernatural. Whether or not this involved anything other than the mind's awareness of its own subconscious need not concern us here. All that matters is that certain herbs, by their action on the mind, were an aid to mystical experience. Among these herbs were hemlock, mandrake, hemp and opium poppy,

---

* cf. *Ps* li, 7: 'Purge me with hyssop and I shall be clean.'

† In the case of henbane, the witches' herb, the relaxing effect may be due to inhaling its fragrance. Years ago people used to dull the pain from toothache by smoking henbane seeds, a practice not without its dangers.

although it is their anaesthetic use we shall examine first.

In the West our earliest learning on the subject comes from Pedacius Dioscorides, physician to Antony and Cleopatra, who described the soporific virtues of different plants. These, of course, were known to people centuries before him, and in some mythologies the gods themselves are said to have revealed them to suffering humanity.

Of the herbal painkillers, mandrake was the most notorious, although its magical properties were even better known. The true mandrake (*Mandragora officinalis*) belongs to the potato family (*Solanaceae*) and grows in Mediterranean countries where it has always been respected as a potent emetic and purgative. Now rarely prescribed by European herbalists, it is still used in the Middle East where its fruit (Arabic *abou ruhr* – 'the giver of life') is thought to be helpful during pregnancy.

Throughout the Middle Ages a decoction of mandrake root was the only anaesthetic available to people undergoing surgery. Not until the fourteenth century did it fall slightly out of favour, when it was replaced by something called the 'soporific sponge'. A sponge was steeped in a tincture of the juices of mandrake, hemlock, opium, wild lettuce and ground ivy. When needed, it was moistened and given to the patient to inhale. For years this sponge, or variants of it, remained the only way of inducing anaesthesia when surgery was about to be performed.

With the development of modern anaesthetics there is no longer any need for their dubious herbal predecessors. We can only look back with pity at those forced to undergo pre-operative ordeals like this one, dating from the seventeenth century, in which the patient drank the combined juices of poppy, mandrake, hemlock, lettuce, ivy and sea holly, and had a second helping of the mixture poured down his nostrils. No wonder it required a draught of two large onions compounded in vinegar to restore the victim to his senses once the operation was completed!

Of more value in our stressful twentieth century are those herbal simples with just enough narcotic power to induce restful sleep. The two described here are mild and non-addictive.* Mix the herbs so

---

* Dependence on herbs or any other soporific should always be resisted. If, having taken herbs for s x weeks, you stop and find you still cannot sleep, then go to see your doctor.

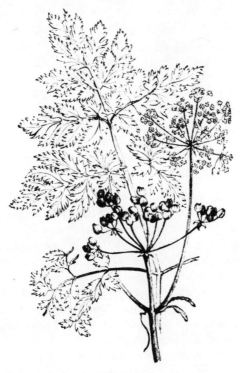

HEMLOCK

as to obtain the usual amount and then prepare the customary standard infusion.

MYDDFAI SLEEPING MIXTURE

red clover heads   *lettuce*

hops

All these herbs have a sound reputation for curing insomnia, and, as I have said, a pillow stuffed with hops is an old-fashioned way of ensuring an undisturbed night. As for the lettuce, it has long been esteemed as a soporific, although its narcotic properties are mild compared with those of its savage cousin, *Lactuca virosa*. Prepare a standard infusion and drink a cupful shortly before retiring.

To increase the strength of this harmless little compound – and only if you really need to – add the ground seed-head of one corn poppy.

LEMNOS WATER

mulberry leaves (Morus niger)	*cowslip leaves*
mullein or *mignonette*	

A wineglassful of the infusion should be drunk before retiring to bed.

The leaves of the *Primulaceae* family of plants (cowslips, primroses, etc.) are noted for their sleep-conducive virtues. Even mulled cowslip wine is said to have the same effect (see p. 65).

There exist other traditional remedies for insomnia, ranging from young puffball mushrooms,* sliced and fried in vegetable oil, to safer-sounding things like nutmeg tea, loosestrife cordial and orange-leaf tisane. The last is still popular on the Continent, where it can be purchased in packets just like ordinary tea. Equally good, it is claimed, is orange tea itself, made by squeezing the juice of two oranges into a cup of sweetened boiling water. Among the French, lime leaves are credited with soporific powers and a *tisane de tilleul* is a fragrant way of calming the nerves before going to rest. As for nutmeg tea, this can easily be prepared by pouring a pint of boiling water over some grated nutmeg, to which you can add a pinch of valerian. This latter herb is not a soporific as such, but it relaxes the mind† and so is useful when worry threatens to rob you of your sleep. Incidentally, if your sleep should ever be disturbed by nasty dreams or nightmares, then a cupful of infused betony will quickly put a stop to them.

So much for the soporific value of these herbs. More interesting is their ability to expand our consciousness and take us outside ourselves.

---

* Care should be taken not to use truffles instead, since these excite the passions. Brillat-Savarin recounts the story of a respectable wife who after eating a fowl stuffed with truffles almost succumbed to the lecherous advances of her husband's best friend. Clearly, they would not be conducive to a peaceful night. (See Brillat-Savarin, *The Philosopher in the Kitchen* [Harmondsworth, Penguin Press, 1970], pp. 92–3.)

† I recall reading that valerian pastilles were handed around among the mourners at Stalin's funeral. Until recently a major airline used to distribute them to its passengers before take-off.

It was this that led the ancients to treasure them as soul medicine capable of giving easy access to a world of numinous experience.

Such herbs were said to be the staple diet of the gods, but their effect on the mortals who ventured to consume them could often be injurious both to sanity and health. This is why their use and even their possession is proscribed in many countries.

Of such herbs the most famous is the poppy, not the corn poppy whose soporific virtues we have noted, but its more exotic relative the white poppy, whose botanical name (*Papaver somniferum*) testifies to its narcotic power. From this graceful plant comes opium, obtained by making incisions in the seed-head, which ripens once the plant has flowered. In time these cuts secrete a gummy juice which is then scraped off and left to dry. Its active ingredient is morphine, which in minute doses serves as a brain stimulant. Bigger doses have the opposite effect (though varying with the addict's tolerance) and tend to dull the brain and induce sleep.

Less dangerous is hashish (from an Arabic word meaning 'dried herb') which comes from the leaves and berries of the Indian hemp plant (*Cannabis indica*). Here the active ingredient is cannabis, variously known as bhang, kif and marijuana, which affects the central nervous system, producing a sense of well-being and enhanced sensory responsiveness. It is a non-addictive drug, although prolonged use of it may promote a psychological dependence among certain people.

Narcotic plants lurk in the most innocent-looking hedgerows. There you will find henbane, one of the many cousins of the mandrake, whose leaves yield a drug called hyoscamine. In minute quantities this drug has a tranquillizing effect, but in excess it causes loss of speech and physical paralysis. Similar dangers attend the careless use of atropine, a drug extracted from deadly nightshade (*Atropa belladonna*). Here the victim lurches from a state of delirious excitement to a deep depression and complete paralysis. Hemlock and other members of its family can be no less damaging (as Socrates found out), and the sea holly, though pleasing to the eye, conceals as we have noted a powerful narcotic in its root. The plant known as monkshood or wolf's bane (*Aconitum lycoctonum*) is also strongly toxic. Plutarch tells how Marc Antony's soldiers went mad after eating the root of this herb, whose poisonous properties were believed to have been the gift of Hecate to whom the entire plant is sacred in witchcraft.

Herbs of this sort were the ingredients of many witches' ointments whose effect was such that those wearing them imagined they could fly through the air to the Sabbat. The wild goings-on at these reunions may likewise have been imaginary; it is known that the plants involved can produce hallucinations. Many and varied were the herbs thus employed, a strange mixture of the good and the baneful. They included devil's claw, wolf's milk, traveller's joy, wormwood, elder, henbane, cornbind and deadly nightshade. A typical witches' ointment was given by Johannes Wierus (1516–88) in his thaumaturgical treatise entitled *De praestigiis daemonum et incantationibus ac veneficiis*. It consists of poison hemlock, poplar leaves, juice of wolf's bane and, of all things, soot. Smeared on the body, it was alleged to confer invisibility on the wearer.

Also growing unnoticed in our hedgerows are other, less toxic, plants whose juices or dried leaves can affect our mental functioning. As with the other more exotic drugs, the effects of taking these vary from one plant – and often one person – to the next: some induce euphoria and a state of 'super-consciousness', others further meditation or increase our sensory enjoyment. Among such herbs are a few that produce hallucinations, and these are often used, in controlled amounts, to develop clairvoyance and other forms of psychism. Unfortunately, even the most well-meaning herbs do harm if taken to excess and, because of the risks involved, I shall refrain from saying much about them here. What I shall do is disclose two traditional recipes which are said to open up the frontiers of the mind without the usual attendant dangers.

WATER OF MAGNANIMITY
mugwort (Artemisia vulgaris)   *loosestrife*
chicory (Cichorium intybus)
Mugwort is a plant held to stimulate the pineal gland,* source of our

---

* The pineal gland, so called because it resembles a miniature pine cone, is situated behind a ventricle of the brain where it grows from the roof of the thalamencephalon. To scientists the precise function of this gland remains a mystery, but occultists describe it as the third eye by means of which clairvoyant impressions are received. Interestingly, the term 'third eye' crops up even among biologists, who tell us that many fish and reptiles have the rudiments of a third eye, complete with lens, just in front of the pineal gland. To this structure the name 'parapineal gland' is sometimes given.

psychic faculties. (Among other things, this gland helps us remember previous incarnations.) The second herb, chicory, has a similar effect but operates on the Tantrist *chakra* Mulhadhara, seat of Kundalini, the 'serpent fire' which, once activated, likewise vivifies the pineal gland. As for loosestrife, it too opens up the 'third eye', just as on the mundane plane, it improves physical vision. (As its name implies, it also relaxes the mind.)

Prepare a standard infusion and drink a glassful after fasting for ten hours and before commencing meditation. The dried leaves may also be smoked.

Tradition has it that these plants are in such sympathy with the magnetic currents of the earth that their leaves turn naturally to the north.

AURA SUAVIS
cornbind (Convolvulus arvensis)   *vervain*
valerian (grated root)
Both valerian and vervain are herbs traditionally associated with the practice of magic, and here they are joined by cornbind, a plant of the same family as morning glory (*Rivea corymbosa*), the flower which enjoyed some notoriety a few years back when young people discovered they could get high on its seeds. This recipe is for a smoking mixture, but the same herbs can be made into a standard infusion provided only a minute quantity of cornbind is included.

Hellenophile occultists prefer laurel leaf to cornbind, claiming that this creates a mixture like that once used by worshippers at Delphi. However, this may well be wishful thinking on their part, and readers who are sceptical and whose tastes are, in any case, more bacchic than delphic may find the next chapter more to their liking.

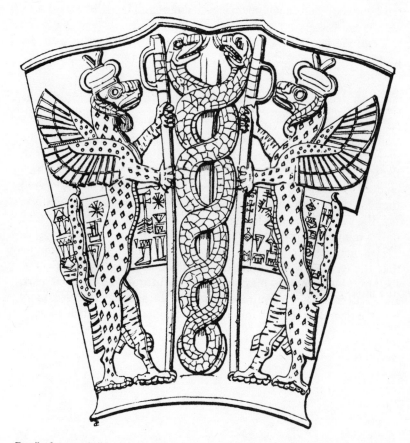

Detail of a vase dedicated to the Sumerian god Ningishzida, the Master Physician, by the King of Babylonia in 2350 B.C. The staff and serpents are still used today in the emblem of the British Medical Association.

7
WINES FROM HERBS
AND FLOWERS

WINES PREPARED from herbs and flowers merit the attention of every herbalist and home wine-maker. Their taste and bouquet subtly reflect the aroma of whatever plant they contain, giving them a special delicate quality not found in other wines. Many have tonic properties as well, but these do not affect their taste, and connoisseurs of fine wines may enjoy them for their own sake and forget about their benefits to health.

The harvesting of plants to be used for making wine demands a certain amount of care, since bruising often harms the flavour of the wine. As when herbs are gathered for medicinal use, a dry day, and preferably a sunny one, should be chosen. In general flower wines are best made from fresh flowers, though dried petals can be used. In the case of other herbal wines it makes little difference whether the ingredients be fresh or dried.

One problem with making wine is that large quantities of plant are sometimes needed to produce several gallons of wine. For that reason it is often easier to buy dried herbs in sachets from a herbalist supplier instead of roaming country lanes in search of them. One of these sachets – costing very little – will normally contain two ounces of herb, sufficient for one gallon of good wine, whereas almost a pound of fresh might be needed.

For the purposes of this chapter I shall give, firstly, the recipes for several wines prepared from fresh flowers and, secondly, the method appropriate when dried herbs are used, illustrating this with a few favourite examples. Naturally all wines must be allowed to ferment, and here the best results can be obtained by using an all-purpose wine yeast.* For sweetening, ordinary white sugar should be used. Wine can be left to ferment quite happily in a warm place, stored in a cloth-covered bottle or, better still, a narrow necked jar fitted with a fermentation lock. (Remove any scum that rises to the top.) A polythene bucket or earthenware crock may also be used, but in that case the container would need to be kept closely covered (but not airtight) to prevent the entry of wild yeasts from the air which would ruin the wine. After the fermentation process is over – and not before – the wine can be siphoned off into bottles and corked. If the wine is still not clear at that stage, the remaining cloudiness will gradually settle in the form of sediment. Before they get this far, however, novice wine-makers are advised to read a book on home-brewing: without due care and caution, home-made wines can all too easily turn into vinegar or worse.

WINES FROM FRESH FLOWERS

CLOVER WINE

3 quarts red clover heads   *1 oz. yeast*
¾ lb. sugar   *1 gal. water*
juice of two lemons

As only the petals are used, pull these away and place them in a suitable container. Pour in two quarts of boiling water and leave the mixture to infuse with a cover over it for ten to twelve hours.

Melt 1½ pounds of sugar in a quart of boiling water, and, when cold, add this syrup to the original infusion. Afterwards add the yeast and lemon juice,† and allow seven days for the first stage of fermentation. At the end of that period, boil the remainder of the sugar in a quart of water and, when cool, add it to the now fermenting mixture. (By adding the sugar in two stages like this, fermentation is prolonged and the maximum alcoholic content thus obtained.) After one day

---

* Old-fashioned wine-makers may still prefer to use baker's yeast, although commercial wine yeast is generally held to make a finer wine with, in addition, a slightly higher alcoholic content.

† The addition of lemon juice compensates for the absence in flowers and herbs of the acid essential to fermentation. Fruit-based wines need no such addition, the natural acid in the fruit being quite sufficient.

strain the liquid and allow the fermentation to continue. This wine is deliciously refreshing on a hot summer's day.

COWSLIP WINE

3 quarts cowslip flowers   *1 oz. yeast*
3 lb. sugar   *1 gal. water*
juice of a lemon or orange (the latter leaves a hint of its flavour)

Place the flower heads in a fermenting-vessel and add four pints of boiling water, leaving this to infuse (under cover) for forty-eight hours.

Boil half the sugar in a quart of water and, when cold, pour this into your jar, adding yeast and the juice of a lemon or orange. Leave the liquid to ferment for four days, and on the fifth strain it and allow it seven more days of fermentation. (A second straining may be needed in this time.) Boil the rest of the sugar in a quart of water and, when cooled, add it to the mixture. The fermentation process can then be left to continue undisturbed.

GORSE WINE

Follow the same procedure as for cowslip wine, using gorse flowers.

DANDELION WINE

1 gal. dandelion heads (insect-free!)   *1 oz. yeast*
3 lb. sugar   *1 gal. water*
juice of 2 lemons

Use only the petals, and place these in a fermenting-vessel, adding two quarts of boiling water and leaving the mixture to infuse for six days. (Again, keep the liquid covered.) On the seventh day strain the infusion and, having boiled half the sugar in a quart of water and let it cool, add this to your mixture. Add also the yeast and lemon juice, leaving the lot to ferment for a week. At the end of that period, strain the liquid and add a further quart of sugar solution.

Leave until you see that all fermentation has stopped.

COLTSFOOT WINE

As above, except that coltsfoot flowers are used. This wine, served hot, is a cordial restorative during convalescence and will also arrest coughing.

HAWTHORN WINE

The method of preparation is again identical to that for making dandelion wine, but only half the quantity of flowers is required. (More than that and the wine tastes sickly sweet.) Country folk maintain that this beverage does the heart much good, and certainly hawthorn is a proven cardiac tonic.

For details of hawthorn nectar, see p. 113.

ELDER FLOWER WINE

1 gal. elder flowers	*½ lb. raisins (stoned and chopped)*
3–3½ lb. sugar	*1 oz. yeast*
juice of 1 lemon	*1 gal. water*

Boil together the water and sugar for five minutes, removing any scum that rises to the surface. Pour this water over the elder flowers and raisins, stirring the mixture well before allowing it to cool. Add the yeast and lemon juice, and leave the liquid to ferment for five days, after which it should be strained and left to ferment in peace.

For a very special wine my mother used to add an egg-cupful of brandy to the wine once it had fermented.

NETTLE BEER

1 gal. nettles	*1 oz. hops*
1½ lb. malt	*1 oz. yeast*
1 lb. sugar	*1 gal. water*
2 oz. sarsaparilla	

Boil the nettles and malt in the water for some thirty minutes, stirring in the sugar, hops and sarsaparilla. Let the liquid stand until it becomes cool enough to add the yeast. Allow it then to ferment in the usual way.

Some authorities suggest that to give zest to the end-product you should bottle the liquid while it is still active. In that case be sure to keep the bottles loosely corked for some time afterwards.

ROSE PETAL DELIGHT

6 pints rose petals (briar rose,	*juice of 2 lemons*
dog rose or well-scented garden	*1 oz. yeast*
blooms)	*1 gal. water*
3 lb. sugar	

Using two quarts of water, infuse the petals for two to three days in a covered container; then add the sugar solution (see previous recipes). The yeast and lemon juice are added next, and the liquid allowed to ferment for ten days, being strained on the sixth day and, if necessary, again on the ninth. Add the remainder of the sugar solution, as before, and leave until fermentation has ceased. This charming wine is said to chase away depression. Some even believe that if only red roses are used in its preparation this beverage mends a broken heart.

ROSE-HIP WINE

5 lb. ripened rose-hips   *1 oz. yeast*
3½ lb. sugar   *1 gal. water*
juice of 1 orange (optional)

The crushed or finely diced hips are left to infuse overnight in the usual two quarts of water. Add the yeast and sugar as before and strain

WILD ROSE

thoroughly after seven days of fermentation. The rest of the sugar can afterwards be added and fermentation allowed to proceed. The result is a delicious wine.

Rose-hip syrup is not difficult to make, but it is probably cheaper and far less trouble to buy it from a chemist's shop.

WINES FROM DRIED HERBS

There is a standard procedure for making herbal wines which is suitable for each of the recipes listed below. To begin with, you should prepare an infusion, using two quarts of boiling water and whatever quantity of herbs is indicated. Allow this infusion to stand, protected from the air, for nine hours. Next, boil half the recommended amount of sugar in a quart of water and, *while it is still boiling*, add this to the rest. Stir the mixture thoroughly, re-cover and, once it has cooled, add the yeast and nutrient.* For the next nine days, leave the liquid to ferment but do try to stir it at least once daily. On the tenth day boil the remainder of the sugar and, *when this has cooled*, add it to the newly strained liquid. Thereafter allow fermentation to continue unimpeded.

Many wine-makers, seeking extra body for their herbal wines, add raisins, wheat and nuts to the other ingredients. Others add a dash of aniseed or liquorice when the wine is nearly ready. While all this is clearly a matter of individual taste, it is generally agreed that herbal wines on their own, though full of flavour and aroma, sometimes lack the panache of fruit-based wines. For that reason I have included raisins in some of the following recipes, particularly where the herb in question is inclined to mildness.

BALM WINE

3 oz. balm leaves   *1 oz. yeast and nutrient*
juice of 2 lemons   *1 gal. water*
3 lb. sugar

I have known people add violets and flowering sprigs of heather ($\frac{1}{2}$ oz.) to this recipe.

---

* Yeast nutrients are substances which, by assisting the yeast to reproduce, accelerate the fermentation process. They are not essential, but their use is advisable with dried herbs. They can be bought quite cheaply from pharmacies and wine-makers' suppliers.

BROOM WINE

3 oz. broom flowers	*2 lb. sugar*
juice of 1 orange and 1 lemon	*1 oz. yeast and nutrient*
1 lb. chopped raisins	*1 gal. water*

Country people believe that broom wine flushes out the kidneys and thus benefits the renal system.

PARSLEY WINE

2 oz. parsley	*½ lb. chopped raisins*
1 oz. mint	*3 lb. sugar*
juice of 3 lemons and 1 orange	*1 oz. yeast and nutrient*
pinch of ground cinnamon or ginger	*1 gal. water*

For extra 'kick', add an egg-cupful of vodka after fermentation.

SAGE WINE

2 oz. sage	*3 lb. sugar*
½ oz. mint	*1 oz. yeast and nutrient*
½ oz. rosemary	*1 gal. water*
1 lb. chopped raisins	

VIOLET CREAM

3 oz. violets	*3 lb. sugar*
½ oz. mint	*1 oz. yeast and nutrient*
½ lb. chopped raisins	*1 gal. water*
juice of one lemon	

YARROW WINE

3 oz. yarrow flowers	*3 lb. sugar*
juice of 2 lemons and 1 orange	*1 oz. yeast and nutrient*
2 oz. ground wheat	*1 gal. water*
2 cloves	

Interesting wines can be made from many other herbs besides those that are shown here. However, for their own sake and that of their guests, beginners would do well to stick to the safe, non-poisonous plants described in Chapter 9. The rest can be left to the Borgias!

Fritillary—Hesitation. 'Dare I trust you?'

8

THE LANGUAGE OF
FLOWERS

Up to this point we have dwelt mostly on the medicinal value of
herbs, glancing also at their narcotic and cosmetic properties. Before
we immerse ourselves in the detailed *materia medica* that will enable
every reader to become his own herbalist, let us consider briefly a
rather special use of herbs, now at risk of being forgotten. This is
floragraphy, a somewhat pompous name for a practice that belongs
to a gentler, more romantic age than ours.

Floragraphy is the practical application of flower symbolism, and
has been used by many ancient civilizations. We in the West have
inherited much of our floral symbolism from Egypt, Assyria and the
classical world, but each country has adapted it to some extent, if
only to accommodate its own native herbs and flowers. Among the
first to bestow qualities and meanings to various plants were poets,
priests and mystics from whose musings there gradually grew up a
language of flowers.* Floragraphy is the use of that language.

A glance at this botanical vocabulary shows that lovers lost no time
in making it their own. By choosing the appropriate flowers, knowing
sweethearts found they could express a wide range of sentiments and
moods. In Europe the heyday of flower symbolism occurred during
the Middle Ages, when Courtly Love imposed its ritualized constraints
on ladies and their knightly suitors. Nowadays, however, with the
need for such discretion long since vanished, floral emblems survive

* In his *Herball* (1597), the writer Gerard quaintly declares: 'through their beauty
and variety of colour and exquisite form they do bring to a liberal and gentle mind
the remembrance of honesty, comeliness and all kinds of virtues.'

71

only on a few old-fashioned Valentine cards. Yet it is sad to see this charming language die, and I think it worth preserving in this chapter – even now some readers of sensibility may prefer floral messages to words.

To speak the language of flowers, you must remember that each herb or bloom carries a specific meaning, often a quality like goodness or fidelity, or a mood like pleasure, jealousy or doubt. The same flower can also convey a message more or less related to its meaning. Thus, by exchanging the right flowers it becomes possible for two people to conduct a secret conversation. (On this basis one bouquet can be made to speak volumes.) In cold print some of these messages may seem a shade ridiculous, but it should be borne in mind that they are meant to be *used*, not read. In some cases, too, the quaint language of the message may cause you some amusement, but again remember that the sentiments behind it are as valid and as current today as they ever were.

Acacia – Sacrifice. 'You must wait yet awhile.'
Aconite – Dislike. 'Your attentions are unwelcome.'
Agrimony – Gratitude. 'Please accept my thanks.'
Almond blossom – Hope. 'I am beginning to enjoy your friendship.'
Anemone – Estrangement. 'You no longer appeal to me.'
Angelica – Inspiration. 'Your love is my guiding star.'
Apple blossom – Goodness. 'You are no less good than you are fair.'
Arbutus – Love. 'Please be mine.'
*Asphodel** – Mourning. 'Our love shall endure after death.'
Aster – Regret. 'I am sorry for my rashness, take it not to heart.'
Azalea – Moderation. 'Avoid extremes of speech and action.'

Balm – Fun. 'I was only jesting.'
Balsam – Impatience. 'I cannot wait to see you.'
Basil – Animosity. 'I dislike you intensely.'
Begonia – Warning. 'We are being watched.'
Bell-flower – Morning. 'Meet me tomorrow morning.'
Bindweed – Persistence. 'I cannot accept your answer.'
Bittersweet – Truth. 'I am sincere.'
Blackthorn – Obstacles. 'Problems lie ahead.'

* Like oak, olive, rosemary and cypress, this is a funeral plant.

Bluebell – Loyalty. 'Be assured, I am true.'

Borage – Brusqueness. 'Your attentions only embarrass me.'

Bracken – Enchantment. 'You fascinate me.'

Bramble – Remorse. 'I was too hasty, please excuse me.'

Broom – Devotion. 'I shall be yours for ever.'

Bugloss – Lies. 'You are untrue.'

Bulrush – Haste. 'Be more discreet in future.'

Burdock – Persistence. 'I shall not be discouraged.'

Buttercup – Radiance. 'Your splendour shines like the sun.'

Camellia – Loveliness. 'How radiant is your beauty.'

Camomile – Fortitude. 'I admire your courage. Do not despair.'

Campion – Poverty. 'Though of humble station, I dare to admire you from afar.'

Campion (red only) – Encouragement. 'I should like to know you better.'

Campion (white only) – Evening. 'Let us meet secretly at dusk.'

Candytuft – Diffidence. 'You may address me, but pray be circumspect.'

Canterbury bell (blue) – Faithfulness. 'Be not deceived, I truly love you.'

Canterbury bell (white) – Acknowledgement. 'Your gift arrived and gave great pleasure.'

Carnation (pink) - Encouragement. 'Yes.'

Carnation (red) – Ardour. 'I must see you soon.'

Carnation (white) – Pure devotion. 'A chaste love I offer you.'

Celandine (*lesser*) – Re-awakening. 'Let this token of spring inform you of my love.'

Cherry blossom - Increase. 'May our friendship wax firm and strong.'

Chrysanthemum (bronze) – Amity. 'Friendship, yes. Love, no.'

Chrysanthemum (red) – Requited love. 'I love you also.'

Chrysanthemum (white) – Honesty. 'I trust you completely.'

Chrysanthemum (yellow) – Coolness. 'I belong to another.'

Cineraria – Delight. 'I enjoy being in your company.'

Cinquefoil – Affection. 'I love you as a brother/sister.'

Cistus – Approval. 'Your beauty enchants me.'

Clarkia – Pleasure. 'Your company delights me.'

Cleavers – Tenacity. 'I shall strive to win your love.'

Clematis – Intelligence. 'I admire your wit and cleverness.'

Clover (pink) – Hurt pride. 'Do not trifle with my affections.'
Clover (red) – Entreaty. 'Will you remain true in my absence?'
Clover (white) – Promise. 'I shall stay faithful.'
Coriander – Hidden qualities. 'Do not judge by appearances alone.'
Cornflower – Delicacy. 'Hurry not, my heart will not be taken by storm.'
Cowslip – Charm. 'You are sweeter than this flower.'
Crocus – Youthful joy. 'My heart rejoices in you.'
Currant – Presumption. 'You and I have nothing in common.'
Cyclamen – Indifference. 'Your declaration leaves me unaffected.'

Daffodil – Rebuttal. 'I do not share your feelings.'
Dahlia (red) – Dismissal. 'You have presumed too much.'
Dahlia (white) – Rebuff. 'Keep away.'
Dahlia (yellow) – Distaste. 'Your attentions are not to my liking.'
Daisy – Delay. 'Await my answer in a few days.'
Daisy (Michaelmas) – Adieu. 'Do not communicate again. I cannot love you.'
Dandelion – Absurdity. 'I find your presumption laughable.'
Deadly nightshade – Deception. 'I do not trust you.'
Dog rose – Purity. 'You are as pure as this sweet flower.'

Eglantine – Sweetness. 'The fragrance of this flower brings memories of you.'
Everlasting flower – Farewell. 'As you request it, leave I must. But I shall never forget you.'

Fern (maidenhair) – Virginity. 'I am yours completely.'
Feverfew – Protection. 'Let me take care of you.'
Flax (blue) – Gratitude. 'I am touched by your kindness.'
Fool's parsley – Folly. 'Let us not be silly, we can still be friends.'
Forget-me-not – Remembrance. 'Think of me often.'
Foxglove – Fickleness. 'Your love is shallow.'
Fraxinella – Ardour. 'My heart is afire.'
Fritillary – Hesitation. 'Dare I trust you?'
Fuschia – Warning. 'Take heed, your lover is false.'
Fumitory – Anger. 'I have expelled you from my thoughts.'

Gardenia – Sweetness. 'This pure flower resembles yourself.'
Geranium (pink) – Doubt. 'I await your explanation.'
Geranium (red) – Duplicity. 'Begone. I cannot trust you.'

Cistus—Approval.
'Your beauty enchants me.'

Tiger lily—Passion.
'My love knows no bounds.'

Geranium (white) – Indecision. 'My mind is not made up.'

Gladiolus – Pain. 'Your slights have wounded me.'

Golden rod – Indecision. 'Allow me time to decide.'

Guelder rose – Young love. 'I want a youthful lover, not one already in his dotage.'

Harebell – Resignation. 'I accept your decision but shall love you still.'

Hart's-tongue fern – Gossip. 'Curb your busy tongue.'

Hawthorn – Hope. 'Despite your answer, I shall strive for your love.'

Heartsease – see Pansy.

Heliotrope – Devotion. 'You are the light of my life.'

Hellebore – Mendacity. 'Do not believe anything until you have heard my explanation.'

Hemlock – Scandal. 'I am unjustly arraigned.'

Herb Paris – Betrothal. 'With this flower I pledge my love.'

Herb Robert – Steadfastness. 'I am yours, come what may.'

Holly – Recovery. 'I am pleased you are restored to health.'

Hollyhock – Ambition. 'Together we can achieve much.'

Honesty – Frankness. 'I have told you everything.'

Honeysuckle – Love. 'With this I plight my troth.'

Hyacinth (blue) – Dedication. 'I shall devote my life to you.'

Hyacinth (white) – Admiration. 'I esteem you highly.'

Hydrangea – Fickleness. 'You change your mind too often.'

Iris (purple) – Ardour. 'My heart is aflame.'

Iris (yellow) – Sorrow. 'I share your sadness.'

Ivy – Tenacity. 'I want you above all else.'

Jasmine – Elegance. 'I admire your poise.'

Jonquil – Petition. 'Please answer soon. Dare I hope you love me?'

Laburnum – Neglect. 'Have you forgotten me?'

Larkspur – Vagueness. 'Give me a definite answer soon.'

Lavender – Sad refusal. 'I like you, but only as a friend.'

Lilac (purple) – Spring love. 'You are my first sweetheart.'

Lilac (white) – Innocence. 'An emblem of your purity and beauty.'

Lily (tiger) – Passion. 'My love knows no bounds.'

Lily (white) – Purity. 'I kiss your fingertips.'

Lily-of-the-valley – Modest detachment. 'Friendship is sweet, talk not of love.'

Lobelia (blue) – Rebuff. 'I do not like you. How, then, can I love you?'

Lobelia (white) – Dislike. 'Your attentions fail to move me.'

London Pride – Flirtation. 'Forgive me for letting you believe I loved you.'

Loosestrife (purple) – Forgiveness. 'Accept this flower as a token of regret.'

Love-in-a-mist – Doubt. 'Your message was unclear. Tell me what you mean.'

Love-lies-bleeding – Broken heart. 'Your refusal robs life of all meaning.'

Lupin – Over-assertiveness. 'Do not rush things.'

Madder – Scandal. 'What you have heard is a cruel lie.'

Magnolia – Courage. 'Be not disheartened, better days are due.'

Marigold – Jealousy. 'You have no reason to feel jealous.'

Marjoram – Maidenly innocence. 'Your passion sends blushes to my cheeks.'

Meadowsweet – Uselessness. 'I seek more than just a pretty face.'

Mignonette – Stolid virtues. 'A worthy jewel but lacking lustre.'

Mimosa – Sensitivity. 'You are too forward.'

Mint – Homeliness. 'Find a spouse of your own age and background.'

Mistletoe – Sweet kisses. 'I send you kisses galore.'

Mullein – Friendship. 'Come, let us be friends.'

Musk – Artificiality. 'Let your natural charms shine through.'

Myrtle – Fragrance. 'Be my love.'

Narcissus – Self-love. 'You love none save yourself.'

Nasturtium – Affectation. 'I prefer natural looks and charm.'

Nettle – Coolness. 'You have offended me.'

Oak leaves – Courage. 'Take heart, love will have its way.'

Oleander – Warning. 'Someone has betrayed us.'

Orange blossom – Virginity.

Orchid – Luxury. 'I shall make your life a sweet one.'

Pansy (purple) – Memories. 'I treasure thoughts of happy times together.'

Pansy (white) – Loving thoughts. 'You are never absent from my mind.'

Pansy (yellow) – Souvenirs. 'Oceans part us but my heart stays with you.'

Passion-flower – Denial. 'I am pledged to another.'

Pelargonium – Acquaintance. 'Talk of friendship not of love.'

Peony – Contrition. 'Forgive my thoughtlessness.'

Periwinkle – First love. 'My heart was mine until we met.'

Petunia – Proximity. 'Stay beside me.'

Phlox (pink) – Friendship. 'I hope we can be friends.'

Phlox (white) – Awakening interest. 'Tell me more about yourself.'

Pimpernel – Meeting. 'Suggest when and where to meet.'

Pink – Fragrance. 'How sweet you are.'

Poppy (red) – Moderation. 'I shall not be rushed. Take time.'

Poppy (white) – Indecision. 'My mind is not made up.'

Primrose – New love. 'I may learn to love you. It's too soon to tell.'

Rest-harrow – Difficulties. 'Obstacles crowd our path.'

Rocket – Competition. 'You are not without a rival.'

Rose (moss) – Timid love. 'I watch you from afar.'

Rose (red) – Love. 'I love you.'

Rose (white) – Refusal. 'I love you not.'

Rose (yellow) – Misplaced affection. 'I love another.'

Rosemary – Remembrance. 'Your memory will never fade.'

Salvia (red) – Passionate love. 'Ardour burns out fast and leaves behind but ashes.'

Saxifrage – Humility. 'One smile from you is worth a fortune.'

Scabious – Misunderstanding. 'You are wrong. I care only a little for you.'

Snapdragon – Refusal. 'You mean nothing to me.'

Snowdrop – Renewal. 'I make a fresh bid for your affection.'

Sunflower – Showiness. 'Outward pomp does not impress me.'

Sweet-gale – Encouragement. 'I like you a little, possibly more.'

Sweet-pea – Tenderness. 'Your memory lingers on.'

Sweet-sultan – Happiness. 'A token to wish you joy.'

Sweet-William – Flirtation. 'My intentions were not serious.'

Tansy – Refusal. 'Your feelings are not reciprocated.'

Thrift – Interest. 'Tell me more.'

Thyme – Homely virtues. 'I need a good home-maker like you.'

Toad-flax – Hesitation. 'Treat me gently.'

Traveller's Joy – Mature love. 'Though youth has gone, my love is strong.'

Trumpet flower – Fire. 'My heart burns with passion.'

Tuberose – Injury. 'Love's flame has singed my wings.'

Tulip – Confession. 'With this flower I declare my love.'

Valerian – Concealed merit. 'Though lowly, I aspire to love you.'

Veronica – True love. 'Nothing shall come between us.'

Vervain – Enchantment. 'You have bewitched me.'

Violet – Modesty. 'As pure as this sweet flower are you.'

Wallflower – Constancy. 'Whatever befalls me, I shall stay true.'

Wormwood – Sorrowful parting. 'Even the best of friends must say farewell.'

To add to the efficacy of floral communication, certain flowers were attributed to different times of the day, thus enabling lovers to arrange their secret meetings without hindrance. A typical floral clock is reproduced below, but seasonal variations of it were often agreed between the two persons involved.

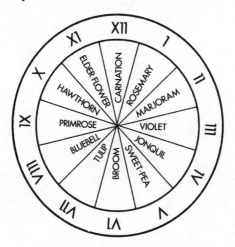

Spring Floral Clock

Also important were the flowers used in conjunction with this clock to convey details of the intended rendezvous. Again, the actual flowers employed were subject to variation, but the following will illustrate how the system worked.

'Let us meet' – pimpernel. 'I can meet you' – pimpernel and clover. 'Tonight' – ivy. 'Today' – lavender. 'Tomorrow' – buttercup. 'I cannot meet you' – pimpernel and daisy. 'Suggest a different time' – pimpernel and plantain. 'Meet me tomorrow at five o'clock' – pimpernel, buttercup, sweet-pea.

As you will see, the success of these exchanges depended on prior collusion between the two star-crossed lovers. Even so, one can well imagine the mishaps that must have arisen from time to time when people got their flowers mixed up or could not lay their hands on the very ones they wanted. Modern lovers have every reason to be grateful for the telephone.

1. VALERIAN *Valeriana officinalis*; 2. SORREL *Rumex acetosa*
3. VIPER'S BUGLOSS *Echium vulgare*; 4. VERVAIN *Verbena officinalis*
5. BUGLE *Ajuga reptans*; 6. THISTLE

9

HERBAL
MATERIA MEDICA

IN THIS chapter you will find an alphabetical list of herbs, most of them common to all temperate regions. A few come from warmer climates, however, and in their case an appropriate reference will always be made in the text. Fortunately almost every one of the plants listed should be available, ready dried, from any good herbal stockist or health food store. This means that no reader need despair if the plant he requires is not one that happens to grow locally. As for those green-fingered readers who have gardens, they will soon find that many of their favourite herbs can be successfully cultivated. Other readers will wish to go out into the countryside to fetch their own herbs, and to them I must stress the need for correct identification. Limitations of space have permitted me to give here but the briefest description of each plant. In doubtful cases, therefore, readers are advised to consult a botanical textbook and, for ease of reference, I have included each herb's botanical title in addition to its commonest English name.

In describing the medicinal use of these herbs I have endeavoured to avoid medical jargon as much as possible. While this makes the general description easier to understand, it nevertheless carries with it a grave risk of over-simplification. It should be emphasized, therefore, that a qualified practitioner is the first person to see if you suspect there is something seriously wrong with your health. With that important caveat in mind, let us discover what herbs have to offer by way of self-medication.

AGRIMONY
Agrimonia eupatoria
Family: *Rosaceae*

This pretty herb grows abundantly by roadsides, at field edges and on wasteland. Its thin hairy stems reach a height of two to three feet, and they bear long slender leaves. The plant flowers in July, and its golden, star-shaped flowers have a mild apricot scent.

Agrimony is of great value in the treatment of dry coughs, where its effect is gently sedative. Some forms of rheumatism, likewise, respond to its action and,

AGRIMONY *Agrimonia eupatoria*

being a Jupiterian plant, it has long been esteemed as a liver tonic. (It is sometimes known as liverwort.) To take this herb, prepare a standard infusion and drink a wineglassful three times daily.

ALDER
Alnus glutinosa
Family: *Betulaceae*

The alder grows near water, where it can be assured of moist soil. It is thus commonly found on riversides and marshy ground. It has shiny oval leaves.

Alder leaf enjoys the reputation of curing dropsical conditions caused by disorders of the renal system. To this end, it is taken in a standard infusion.* The same

ALDER *Alnus glutinosa*

infusion may also be used as a lotion for cooling sore, tired feet. It is even claimed that an alder leaf placed in each shoe will prevent fatigue when walking. (The Myddfai doctors prefer a mugwort leaf for this.)

* Again, where no dosage is specified, follow the dosage recommended on p. 36.

ANGELICA
Angelica officinalis
Family: *Umbelliferae*

A large aromatic plant growing wild (*Angelica sylvestris*) and in gardens (*Angelica archangelica*), angelica has downy, triangular leaves. Above these the hollow stalk branches out, each branch bearing a compound umbel of white or, more rarely, pale-purple flowers.

ANGELICA *Angelica officinalis*

Angelica is above all a herb for the digestion, bringing swift relief from flatulence, colic and heartburn. An infusion should be made from the leaves and chopped stem. This will also provide an excellent gargle for the treatment of sore tonsils and throats. Angelica has general tonic properties and is a pleasant herb to take. Its raw stalks, for example, are delicious when eaten with a little cream cheese, and the washed roots are also quite tasty. This plant is used to flavour many alcoholic drinks and its candied stem has long been used in confectionery.

BALM *Melissa officinalis*

BALM
Melissa officinalis
Family: *Labiatae*

A fragrant woodland plant with dark-green wrinkled leaves and small creamy flowers, its virtues have been known since the very earliest times. The great Paracelsus called this herb the elixir of life, and combined it with carbonate of potash in a mixture known as *Primum Ens Melissae*. It is recorded that one of Louis XIV's physicians, Lesebure, tried this out on an elderly chicken, which within a few days lost its tattered plumage, grew fresh feathers and started to lay eggs again.*

For centuries this tonic herb has been prescribed in cases of nervous trouble, and it is also a celebrated treatment for many female disorders, including infertility and menstrual irregularity. As it promotes sweating, balm is a valuable stand-by when fever is present. Its leaves – they have a lemony taste – are best eaten raw – a few daily – but a standard infusion may also be prepared.

Eau de Carmes, a fashionable seventeenth-century perfume, was a distillation of balm leaves and spirits of wine, to which were added lemon peel, nutmeg, cloves and cinnamon. Balm oil is still a favourite scent throughout the Middle East.

BARBERRY *Berberis vulgaris*

BARBERRY
Berberis vulgaris
Family: *Berberidaceae*
A pretty shrub whose drooping chains of yellow flowers brighten many woods and hedges. Its leaves are edged with spiky teeth and the red oblong berries – each about $\frac{1}{2}$ in. long – grow in copious clusters.

The chopped bark and, when available, the berries are the parts commonly used in medicine. Both have a salutary effect on the liver and spleen and can be used to treat associated conditions. Prepare a standard decoction.

More delicious is barberry conserve, something every home jam-maker should be able to manage quite easily.

* He had earlier tried it, with equally dramatic results, on two old servants, but did not complete the experiment (see Lesebure, *Chemischer Handleiter* [1685], p. 276). Another of Paracelsus's elixirs, the *Primum Ens Sanguinis*, contained human blood and Alcahest, a universal medicine based on caustic lime, alcohol and carbonate of potash.

Barley

Hordeum pratense
Family: *Gramineae*

Barley grows wild in many damp places but is for the most part cultivated. Its leaves are broader than many other grasses, but more characteristic still is the 'bearded' look of its spikes, this being due to the long awns that grow from them. A field of ripened barley is a beautiful sight and seems to radiate a pale yellow light.

Apart from its nutritional value (it is, among other things, rich in

BARLEY *Hordeum pratense*

iron and vitamin B), barley has sound medicinal virtues: it cools the body, strengthens the nerves and remedies many disorders. In addition, barley water is widely prescribed for a variety of bladder and kidney ailments. Needless to say, the nutritional and medicinal properties of barley combine to make it an excellent tonic food during convalescence. (Prepare a gruel and flavour to taste.) Barley bread can also be bought at health food shops and good bakeries.

BASIL *Ocimum basilicum*

Basil

Ocimum basilicum
Family: *Labiatae*

An aromatic herb that tends to favour sunny banks, basil is now widely cultivated and obtainable from any herbalist supplier. Its white flowers grow in whorls, and the leaves are oval-shaped and shiny. The scent of basil is conducive to meditation, and the plant is often used in magic.

Medicinally, basil is a potent tonic whose effect is both stimulant and nervine, a rare com-

85

bination, since nerve herbs are generally sedative. An efficient settler of the digestion, basil will quell the most violent vomiting and nausea. (It is, incidentally, particularly good at arresting morning and travel sickness.) A sprig of basil in the wardrobe will keep moths and other insects at bay.

To take this herb, prepare a standard infusion from the leaves.

BETONY *Betonica officinalis*

BETONY
Betonica officinalis
Family: *Labiatae*

This purple-flowered plant frequents woodlands and dense hedges, where it always craves the shade. Traditionally the herb comes under the patronage of Jupiter, and astrologically-minded herbalists gather it on a Thursday, if possible when the moon has set in Libra. Here we have a fine natural painkiller, especially good for headaches and neuralgia. The chief fame of betony, however, derives from its tonic properties, which are of special value to the nervous system. Older herbals claim that it purifies the blood and prescribe it in cases of acne. A standard infusion is made from the whole herb and anything from a teaspoonful to a small cupful taken up to three times daily.

Betony was a favourite herb of the Saxons, others being mugwort, sage and valerian. Fresh betony leaf was believed to prevent drunkenness if chewed before a party, and, as a nightcap, an infusion is supposed to keep away bad dreams.

86

BIRCH
Betula alba
Family: *Betulaceae*

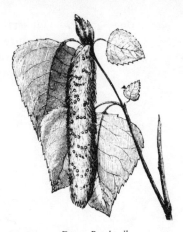

BIRCH *Betula alba*

Birch leaves have always been successful in the treatment of skin complaints, including obdurate cases of acne, pruritis and eczema. A standard infusion is generally prepared and one wineglassful taken each morning on rising. If available, the juice of the bark can be applied direct to the skin, but take care to ensure no dirt is present. Alternatively, an essential oil of the bark may be prepared for external use, but this is too greasy for treating acne and other oily skin conditions. It can, however, be used to relieve rheumatic and allied pains.

BISTORT
Polygonum bistorta Family: *Polygonaceae*
A meadow plant with pale pink flowers, bistort is second to none in soothing sore throats. While most antibiotics kill germs good and bad, this herb removes all local discomfort and lets the body fight its own battle. To prepare the herb, a decoction is made from the root, and this may be drunk or used as a mouthwash or gargle. It is often claimed that bistort will heal internal ulcers.

BLACKBERRY
Rubus fruticosus Family: *Rosaceae*
All readers will be familiar with this shrub, whose berries are not only delicious but good for anaemia as well. Country folk have long used a decoction of blackberry root to curb diarrhoea in children. The leaves, on the other hand, are mildly aperient and accredited with sound tonic virtues. A standard infusion is made, which can also be applied externally as a lotion, when it is reported to cure psoriasis and scaly conditions of the skin.

No less beneficial is the black currant (*Ribes nigrum*) whose leaves, in an infusion, will remedy catarrhal disorders of the chest. The berries are extraordinarily rich in vitamin C.

BLACKBERRY *Rubus fruticosus*

BOG MYRTLE *Myrica gale*   BORAGE *Borago officinalis*   BROOM *Cytisus scoparius*

BOG MYRTLE
Myrica gale Family: *Myricaceae*

An aromatic plant that favours damp soil, bog myrtle, or sweet gale as it is sometimes called, will be found on moors, marshes and fens. Its leaves are dull green, almost grey, and grow somewhat sparsely from a brownish stem. The flowers, catkin-like and pink, are followed by bright orange berries.

The leaves of this herb are the part used. Though bitter, they may be chewed raw or used to prepare a standard infusion. Bog myrtle is a good general tonic and restorative, of special value during bouts of sickness, depression or strain. It quickly revives the spirit, quickens the mind and strengthens the nerves. Cases of poor memory and mental confusion in old age are successfully treated with this plant.

BORAGE
Borago officinalis Family: *Boraginaceae*
Its brilliant blue flowers are the distinctive feature of this woodland and pasture plant. It grows to a height of almost two feet, and both leaves and stem are covered with whitish bristles.

Borage has a beneficial effect on the heart, kidneys, adrenal glands and entire digestive system. In addition, it is famous as a curer of jaundice. In all cases a cupful of the infused herb should be drunk night and morning.

This herb increases the milk flow in nursing mothers, but still better for that purpose is the aptly named milkwort (*Polygala vulgaris*), a tiny plant that should ideally be eaten raw but can also be drunk as a tisane (two cupfuls daily). Excessive milk flow can be checked by taking periwinkle.

Borage juice, obtained from the crushed plant and applied direct to the skin, will destroy ringworm.

BROOM
Cytisus scoparius Family: *Papiloniaceae*
A familiar shrub found on heaths and hillsides, and comprising several erect green branches from which oval leaflets grow. (Unlike gorse, with which it is sometimes confused, broom rarely sports any prickles.) It flowers from April to June, and its bright yellow flowers are much favoured by butterflies. Broom is one of the nine fairy herbs, and a cologne prepared from its flowers is said to inspire affection.

Broom is a peerless lymph tonic and is instrumental in curing many cases of dropsy, being mildly diuretic as well. (Its active ingredient is an alkaloid, spartein sulphate.) The tops of young branches should be picked, and an infusion made using three dessertspoonfuls of herb to three-quarters of a pint of water. Alternatively, a decoction can be prepared from the root. The correct dosage in both cases is a tablespoonful night and morning.

BUGLE
Ajuga reptans Family: *Labiatae*
Bugle (see p. 80) flourishes everywhere, but is particularly fond of

damp woods and meadows. It has a squarish steam, topped in spring and summer with tight whorls of blue flowers. The leaves from the root are stalked, those from the stem – often tinged with blue – are stalkless.

This refreshing herb is one of the mildest herbal narcotics, and can be prescribed in all cases. It is also a fine digestive, having a sedative influence on upset stomachs. Prepare a standard infusion from the leaves and sweeten with honey.

BURDOCK *Arctium lappa*

BURDOCK
Arctium lappa
Family: *Compositae*
A favourite home of the burdock is the damp soil of ditches and meadows, but it will make do with any waste land it can find. Country children know it for the sport they can get from its prickly fruit heads, which stick to the clothes.

As a cordial restorative burdock has few close rivals, and older herbalists still prescribe it as a 'blood tonic'. Certainly it does put pep into the circulation on a cold winter's morning. (But take care, for the herb is diuretic and that, plus the chill weather, may well complicate the rest of your day!) It is also recommended for the treatment of arthritis and rheumatism.

Prepare a standard infusion, or else make a decoction from the sliced root. Used externally, either preparation provides a soothing skin and scalp lotion, once thought to cure leprosy. It should be noted that the seeds of this herb are good for sciatica: they may be chewed, or ground fine and taken with a little jam or honey.

BURNET
Sanguisorba officinalis Family: *Rosaceae*
This plant dislikes high ground, preferring instead the moister soil of low, sheltered valleys. It has juicy leaves, and round clusters of

small purplish flowers.

The botanical name of this herb (Latin *sanguis* = blood) refers to its ability to staunch bleeding from wounds. For this purpose, pound the leaves into pulp and spread on a clean piece of bandage or lint. To prevent haemorrhaging, prepare a standard infusion from the whole herb above ground. This infusion will also regulate many disorders of the blood, promote the healing of wounds and cure most skin ailments (internal and external use). The same

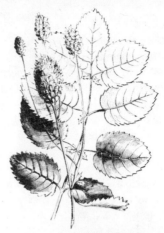

BURNET *Sanguisorba officinalis*

beverage has cooling and tonic properties, as have fresh burnet leaves, which may be added to all summer salads. Another species of burnet actually goes by the name of salad burnet (*Poterium sanguisorba*). An infusion provides a refreshing tonic, especially in hot weather, and it was once used to make beer.

BUTTERBUR *Petasites vulgaris*

BUTTERBUR
Petasites vulgaris
Family: *Compositae*
This thick-stalked plant appears early in the spring. A little later come the flowers, preceding the leaves and gathered in dense pinkish clusters. (Bees love them for their nectar.) The leaves themselves are kidney-shaped, rough-toothed and large (often as many as three feet in diameter). Their undersides are white.

Butterbur is a general tonic, stimulating the heart, especially, and because of its mild diuretic effect benefiting the kidneys. It is a popular ingredient in many herbal tonics. The root is the part used, and a standard decoction is prepared.

CAMOMILE
Anthemis nobilis
Family: *Compositae*
Found in many waste places, camomile is a very familiar weed, having daisy-like flowers and feathery grey-green leaves. The whole plant has a distinctive smell, reminiscent of over-ripe apples. Amateur gardeners will have heard of camomile lawns, their attraction being that they not only wear well but smell sweetly when trodden on.

CAMOMILE *Anthemis nobilis*

An infusion of the leaves and flowers of this plant, fresh or dried, has a wide variety of uses: it dissolves tumours, heals ulcers, expels worms, banishes tiredness and generally revives the system. For centuries country folk have relied on camomile to cure children's complaints and to treat many female disorders. This herb has its cosmetic uses too: as a face-wash, the standard infusion will clarify the complexion, and, as a rinse, will lighten fair hair. Camomile tea is tonic, digestive and tranquillizing. Some people prefer it when it is sweetened with honey.

CANDYTUFT *Iberis amara*

CANDYTUFT
Iberis amara
Family: *Cruciferae*
Liking dry chalky soil, this plant has dark shiny leaves and tufts of creamy white flowers. Once an inmate of every self-respecting herb garden, it has now lost a little of its popularity. This is a pity since it is an excellent herb for rheumatic complaints. I have great faith in it, having witnessed its success in relieving the most

chronic cases of arthritis. A standard infusion is prepared from all parts of the plant above ground. To sustain the treatment, chew some candytuft seeds at intervals during the day.

CATNIP
Nepeta cataria
Family: *Labiatae*

A common inhabitant of hedges and waste places, catnip has a downy stem which at the height of summer bears a spike of white or lilac-coloured flowers. These are small and hooded, and grow in crowded whorls. As its name suggests, cats are very partial to the curious scent of this plant. They and other creatures eat it for its medicinal virtues, and early herbalists, observing this, were quick to add it to their treasury of simples.

Above all a digestive herb, catnip relieves all stomach cramps, flatulence and intestinal pain. It expels wind and reduces discomfort without impeding the normal digestive processes. An anti-spasmodic, it is used in Wales to stop persistent coughs and hiccups. Elsewhere I have seen it prescribed as a safe yet efficient painkiller, especially suitable for children's aches and pains. The dosage is one or two tablespoonfuls daily of the standard infusion, which is prepared from the whole plant above ground. Painful menstruation is relieved with this herb which will also induce restful sleep if taken before going to bed.

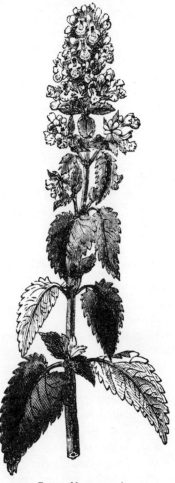

CATNIP *Nepeta cataria*

CELANDINE (GREATER)
Chelidonium majus Family: *Papaveraceae*

Found in hedgerows and wastes, this member of the poppy family
has no connection with its better known namesake, the lesser celandine,
a cousin of the buttercup. The greater celandine has hairy leaves
shaped like oak-leaves, yellowish in colour, and small yellow flowers.

As a wart cure the raw yellow juice should be applied direct to the
skin, but care must be taken as this juice is rather toxic. Some herbals
describe an eye lotion made from one part of the infused herb and
two parts of water or milk, but I myself have never tried it.*

GREATER CELANDINE *Chelidonium majus*   LESSER CELANDINE *Ranunculus ficaria*

CELANDINE (LESSER)
Ranunculus ficaria Family: *Ranunculaceae*

The bright yellow flowers of the lesser celandine grace the hedgerow
every spring. Its leaves are heart-shaped and often speckled with
blobs of black or purple. Of more interest is the root, which sprouts
a number of cylindrical tubers; these pile-like nodules were taken
to suggest that the plant might cure haemorrhoids – hence its other
name, the pilewort.

Despite the doubtful reasoning by which this herb's medicinal use
was first discovered, it remains true that an ointment prepared from
the crushed root will stop the discomfort from piles. For extra benefit,
add stonecrop (*Sedum album*) or toadflax to the ointment. The same
preparation will also heal boils, sores and painful whitlows.

* Among the eye herbs not separately listed elsewhere in this section are lady's
mantle (*Alchemilla vulgaris*), lovage (*Ligusticum scoticum*), summer savory (*Satureja
hortensis*) and mugwort (*Artemisia vulgaris*).

CENTAURY
Centaurium vulgare
Family: *Gentianaceae*
Centaury is plentiful along the coast and on some hilly pastures. The leaves are narrow, small and bitter-tasting, the flowers pink and star-shaped.

CENTAURY *Centaurium vulgare*

When I was a small boy, my mother used always to dab the cuts and scratches I acquired with an infusion of centaury flowers. The infusion (which can also be prepared from the leaves) is a first-class wash for wounds and sores, and is strongly antiseptic. (It also makes a good mouth-wash.) I used also to be made to drink a centaury infusion whenever subject to one of my periodic attacks of biliousness and, though not a pleasant herb to take, it certainly did me lots of good. Centaury is, in fact, a potent liver tonic and much favoured by herbalists to treat jaundice and other hepatic disorders.

CHERVIL
Anthriscus sylvestris Family: *Umbelliferae*
This plant, with its filigree leaves and clusters of delicate flowers, grows wild at roadsides and underneath hedges. It is known also as cow parsley. The Romans, who had a great respect for chervil (in this case, *Anthriscus cerefolium*), planted it near their encampments, and it still grows in the vicinity of these ancient sites. Chervil belongs to the family *Umbelliferae*, some of whose members, like the hemlock, are poisonous, and many beginners find it difficult to distinguish true chervil from its more ill-disposed cousins. Fortunately, chervil is again becoming a popular culinary herb and may therefore be bought ready dried at small cost.

The fame of this herb rests upon its tonic properties. It has always been noted as a powerful brain stimulant (I used to take some before school exams). Elderly people find it a useful tonic, especially if their memory has started to fail. Used in a standard infusion, chervil

CHERVIL *Anthriscus sylvestris*   HORSE CHESTNUT *Aesculus hippocastanum*

is also remarkable for its anti-depressant effect. The leaves have a quite pleasant taste and may be eaten fresh in a salad. Otherwise, make a standard infusion.

CHESTNUT (HORSE)
Aesculus hippocastanum Family: *Hippocastanaceae*
Horse-chestnut leaves have marked narcotic tendencies, and a cupful of standard infusion will ensure deep, calm sleep. It should not, however, be taken too often despite the tonic properties it also enjoys. Essence of horse-chestnut is rich in vitamin K and therefore valuable in treating all circulatory disorders. People suffering from poor circulation, piles, varicose veins and chilblains would do well to drink some regularly.

CHICKWEED
Stellaria media
Family: *Caryophyllaceae*

Quick to grow in newly turned soil, chickweed has small, yellowish-green leaves which have long been favoured as an iron-rich tonic for cage birds. This herb affords similar benefits to humans as well, but its more specific medicinal use is in the treatment of stomach ulcers and all forms of internal inflammation. It also aids the digestion.

CHICKWEED *Stellaria media*

The herb may be taken raw, if available, or else in a standard infusion of which a sherry-glassful is drunk thrice daily. The same infusion refines the texture of the skin when applied as a face lotion.

That other canary tonic, groundsel (*Senecio vulgaris*), is also good for mankind, being a popular ingredient of many herbal tonics. (In large doses its effect is emetic, so be careful with it.) Pulped groundsel, used as an eye compress, heals sties and reduces puffiness round the eyes.

CINQUEFOIL
Potentilla reptans
Family: *Rosaceae*

This herb will be found on grassland, waste places and along roadsides. It is a prolific creeper, sometimes confused with wild strawberry. Its long-stalked leaves are composed of five hairy leaflets, and the single flowers are golden-yellow in colour. (The wild strawberry, on the other hand, has small, *white* flowers and trefoil leaves.)

A favourite nerve herb of the

CINQUEFOIL *Potentilla reptans*

gipsies, cinquefoil has a powerfully sedative effect. (Standard infusion of leaves and chopped stem.) It is particularly good in cases of hysteria, epilepsy and, it is said, schizophrenia. It is an excellent painkiller; the infusion may be taken for sore throats and swollen tonsils, and as a gargle it offers fast local relief.

More pleasant-tasting than the standard infusion is cinquefoil cordial, a German speciality, made by infusing three ounces of dried herb (or a handful of fresh) in a litre of hock. Take a wineglassful morning and night.

CLEAVERS *Galium aparine*

CLEAVERS
Galium aparine
Family: *Rubiaceae*
Dense, tangled masses of cleavers can be seen clinging to surrounding vegetation in most of our hedgerows. The plant has tiny white flowers, but more familiar are the small round fruit which bristle with stiff hairs. Indeed, the entire plant is covered with the same tiny spines.

Cleavers are an excellent remedy for many diseases of the urinary system. They are also invaluable in cases of arthritis, fever and jaundice. Moreover, an infusion of this herb, used as a lotion, makes a first-rate tonic for the scalp (which it clears of dandruff) and the skin (it was once held to cure leprosy and is still used to treat skin cancer). Two fistfuls of freshly chopped herb should be infused in a pint of water.

This herb makes an admirable poultice which will reduce cysts, boils and swellings.

COLTSFOOT
Tussilago farfara Family: *Compositae*
Coltsfoot has large heart-shaped leaves and, from March onwards, bright-yellow flowers. It frequents hedges and waste land, and is

COLTSFOOT *Tussilago farfara*

particularly fond of stiff, clayey soil. Traditionally a herb of Venus, it has been said that coltsfoot 'maddens young stallions and fleet-footed mares' (Theocritus, *Idylls*).

This little plant is an ingredient of many herbal cough mixtures, but can also be used on its own to clear the chest and restore a lost voice. It is a powerful expectorant and will also reduce fevers. Prepare a standard infusion and take a tablespoonful as often as required.

Culpeper gives the recipe for a cough mixture consisting of six handfuls of fresh coltsfoot, two of hyssop, two of maidenhair fern and two ounces of liquorice root (*Glycorrhiza glabra*), these to be boiled in four pints of spring water until only three pints remain.

COMFREY
Symphytum officinale
Family: *Boraginaceae*
A plant that likes moisture, comfrey flourishes in ditches and other damp places. Its bell-shaped flowers are a pinkish blue and hang in clusters.

Comfrey was known to the Crusaders as a wound herb, since it is unrivalled in repairing broken bones and battered bodies. It is often combined with boneset (*Eupatorium perfoliatum*). Eye injuries also respond well to its

COMFREY *Symphytum officinale*

99

action. This valuable herb may be taken up to three times daily in an infusion of the leaves or a decoction from the bruised root. Alternatively, a teaspoonful of the fresh juice of the plant may be taken twice daily. For external use, the infusion may be applied locally or a poultice made from the macerated leaves. For eye injuries, prepare a cold compress (which is a poultice applied cold).

CORIANDER
Coriandrum sativum Family: *Umbelliferae*

Coriander, a native of Southern Europe and the Middle East, has long been cultivated in other parts of Europe and in America. It is still grown commercially, but by now grows wild as well on many roadside wastes. Its leaves resemble those of parsley, its cousin, and the flowers are small, pinkish white and borne in umbels. When bruised, coriander has a curious smell which many people dislike, but the herb is quite palatable for all that. Indeed, it is often used in pharmacy to mask the taste of other drugs and in cookery to flavour casseroles and curries.

Medicinally, coriander is an efficient remedy for painful indigestion, a condition it will help to prevent, as well – a few seeds chewed before meals will keep the most fastidious system happy. This herb may be taken in a standard infusion prepared from the leaves or seeds. Also a fine heart tonic, coriander strengthens and improves the functioning of that organ. Among some Arab tribes coriander is highly esteemed as a medicine for women, regulating menstruation and easing labour.

CORNFLOWER *Centaurea cyanus*

CORNFLOWER
Centaurea cyanus
Family: *Compositae*

Found in town and country gardens, this pretty plant still grows wild in some cornfields. It has narrow leaves, and its bright blue flowers are, in form, typical of the rest of the thistle family.

In herbalism, cornflower is extensively used to remedy disorders of the nervous system, being both curative and calming.

I have seen cases where its regular use has cured certain forms of paralysis, particularly the partial sort that often follows strokes. Prepare a standard infusion from the flowers.

Another blessing of this herb is its ability to cure many eye ailments, including even chronic ones. It is even reported to improve the sight. In these cases make a strong infusion and apply as an eye-wash.

COWSLIP
Primula veris
Family: *Primulaceae*

COWSLIP *Primula veris*

Partial to damp, clayey ground, the cowslip grows happily in meadows and pastures. Its tuft of veined, wrinkled leaves resembles that of the primrose, but the cowslip is easily distinguishable by its longer stalks and clusters of yellow funnel-shaped flowers. The latter appear in the spring and are faintly honey-scented.

The cowslip is an effective painkiller and sedative. Make a standard infusion from the leaves and take a cupful as and when needed. (But not *too* often, as the plant is mildly narcotic.) A tea made from the leaves will refresh the nerves and ensure restful sleep.

Cowslip leaves in a cold cream base do much to hinder wrinkles and preserve the complexion.

DAISY
Bellis perennis Family: *Compositae*

So common is our friend the daisy that no description is needed. Its name, derived from the Old English 'daéges eage' (day's eye), refers to its habit of closing its petals by night or during wet weather. (In this way its stigmas are fertilized through contact with the pollen at the yellow centre of the flower.)

The daisy improves the circulation and so helps those who feel the cold or suffer from chilblains. In addition, it keeps the walls of the arteries soft and flexible. A standard infusion should be made from the leaves, the subsequent dosage being two tablespoonfuls daily. The infusion may also be applied externally, as 'daisy water', to clarify the complexion. An ointment prepared from the crushed leaves takes much of the soreness from bruises.

Daisy wine has an unusual taste but is nevertheless very pleasant. To make it, follow the instructions

DAISY *Bellis perennis*

for other flower wines, using 2 quarts daisy heads, $\frac{1}{2}$ gal. water, 2 lb. sugar, juice of 1 lemon and 1 orange, and $\frac{3}{4}$ oz. yeast.

DANDELION
Taraxacum officinale
Family: *Compositae*
As in the case of the daisy, a description is hardly necessary. The golden-yellow flower-heads of this poor, despised plant brighten up fields, hedgerows and many a drab piece of land.

The medicinal value of the dandelion was prized by the Myddfai physicians, who recommended it for the treatment of all kidney complaints, liver trouble and circulatory disorders. It is widely used, too, for treating arthritis; it is said to disperse

DANDELION *Taraxacum officinale*

acidic deposits from the affected joints. To benefit from this herb, the leaves (slightly bitter) should be eaten raw in salads; or, if you prefer, prepare an infusion in the usual way. Quite tasty, but of rather less medicinal worth, is dandelion coffee, made by 'roasting' the washed roots in a warm oven. They are then ground to a fine powder to which pure coffee or chicory root may be added to taste. Finally, the 'milk' from the hollow stalks of this plant may be applied with good effect to all pimples and spots.

DEVIL'S BIT SCABIOUS
Succisa pratensis　Family: *Dipsaceae*
The attentive herbalist will find this plant growing on heaths, meadows and pastures. Its leaves are sparse, grey-green and hairy, its terminal flower-heads sky-blue and sweet scented. If you examine the root you will see that it ends abruptly, where, according to legend, the Devil bit off a chunk in the hope of killing the plant and thus depriving mankind of its benefits.

The flowers, and, of less importance, the leaves, of this herb are used to treat many gynaecic disorders (menstrual, uterine and vaginal). Make a standard infusion and take a tablespoonful three times daily. Long esteemed as an anti-spasmodic nerve tonic, it is also prescribed for the treatment of hysteria, fits and chorea.

ELDER
Sambucus nigra　Family: *Caprifoliaceae*
The elder was always regarded as a magical tree, being an acknowledged affrighter of demons. For this reason undertakers once carried pieces of elder as a protection against the dubious spirits to which their calling exposed them. So revered was this plant that it became unlucky to damage it wantonly. In parts of Europe it was even customary to doff one's hat in its presence and to offer a prayer to the elder mother before gathering her berries. Our ancestors went in fear of this matriarch who, among other things, devoured their children – a reason why cradles were never made of elder wood. In Christian communities the tree increased its sinister reputation since it was thought to be the wood of the Cross. In addition, popular belief supposed it to have been the tree from which Judas Iscariot hanged himself.

Legends apart, the benefits of the elder tree have been acknowledged

ELDER *Sambucus nigra*

since Druidic times and are highly esteemed to this day. All parts of the tree are used, its leaves combining with honey in a standard infusion that clears troubled skin, the infused flowers offering a remedy for catarrh, coughs and colds, and the berries (mildly laxative) soothing all burns and scalds. (In addition, a balm of elder flowers is said to keep crow's feet at bay.) Finally, to prepare an excellent gargle, infuse some elder flowers and a good pinch of sage, add a teaspoonful each of honey, lemon juice and vinegar, strain and allow the mixture to cool to a comfortable temperature.

Also noteworthy is dwarf elder or danewort (*Sambucus ebulus*) whose infused leaves are an efficient cure for dropsy and the localized puffiness associated with that condition.

ELECAMPANE
Inula helenium
Family: *Compositae*
This herb is fairly common in fields and on wastes. Its wrinkled hairy leaves are vivid green and rather 'tacky' to the touch. The flowers are bright yellow and the whole plant exudes a pungent odour.

Elecampane is a chest herb, used to treat asthma, bronchitis and hay fever. It is strongly expectorant and can therefore be prescribed whenever excess

ELECAMPANE *Inula helenium*

mucus must be lifted from the chest. Here its powers are undeniable, but I am less convinced by the claims – often made – about its tonic effect on the lungs. In all cases a standard infusion is prepared.

As a nasal wash or inhalation, elecampane effectively clears catarrh. It is also incorporated in herbal ointments for rheumatic aches and pains.

EYEBRIGHT
Euphrasia officinalis
Family: *Scrophulariaceae*
A tiny meadow herb whose white flowers are edged with mauve and yellow. The leaves are oval-shaped and slightly downy.

As its name suggests, this herb is used to treat ophthalmic complaints and, over the years, many remarkable cures have been attributed to it. Eyebright is often prescribed where the vision has deteriorated and, here again, excellent results are reported. For internal or external treatment, a

EYEBRIGHT *Euphrasia officinalis*

standard infusion is prepared from the whole flowering plant. Apart from its effect on the eyes, the infusion is of value in curing disorders of the spleen, stomach and gall bladder. It will also quell indigestion.

A good eye lotion can be made by adding twenty drops (roughly one teaspoonful) of tincture to half a cup of slightly saline water that has first been boiled and allowed to cool. The eyes are then washed three times daily.

FENNEL
Foeniculum officinale Family: *Umbelliferae*
Since it is used in cooking, fennel can be purchased quite cheaply. Its frail-looking leaves are dark green and have a strong mossy scent. In herbalism they are used to treat rheumatism, cramps, gastric disorders and general debility. They are reputed to improve the memory and, coupled with lily-of-the-valley, provide the ideal

FENNEL *Foeniculum officinale*

FEVERFEW *Matricaria parthenium*

restorative for people recovering from strokes. In all these cases an infusion is made from the leaves. (A similar infusion prepared from the seeds will allay coughing.) The shoots of this plant have a laxative effect and may be consumed raw or as a tisane.

The ancients believed that myopic reptiles ate fennel to improve their vision and so used it themselves for this purpose. It is still prescribed as an eye-wash.

FEVERFEW
Matricaria parthenium
Family: *Compositae*
This aromatic plant has round, yellowish-green leaves and small daisy-like flowers. It grows abundantly in hedgerows, on sunny banks and along the sides of roads.

Feverfew has already been mentioned as one of the herbs traditionally prescribed to treat infertility. Primarily a women's herb, it is capable of, among other things, assisting labour, releasing afterbirth and preventing abortion. In addition to these special uses, feverfew aids the digestion and is mildly aperient. It is also a valuable poultice herb, having cooling and analgesic properties. The pulped herb, leaves, stalk and flowers, may be compounded with bland soap and used to prepare suppositories for the localized treatment of piles. For all internal uses, make the customary infusion.

FIGWORT
Scrophularia nodosa
Family: *Scrophulariaceae*

Found in moist, shady corners, figwort has pointed, heart-shaped leaves, the edges of which are sharply toothed. Throughout the summer its square stem (which reaches a height of three to four feet) bears sparse clusters of greenish-mauve flowers. The plant's most noticeable characteristic, however, is its smell – delightful to insects, but offensive to human beings.

This herb's other name is the throatwort, perhaps because of its reputation in some country districts as a remedy for sore throats and inflamed tonsils. In Wales it is used to treat circulatory disorders, and is especially good

FIGWORT *Scrophularia nodosa*

at reducing varicose veins. (In this case the plant's 'signature' is undoubtedly its own knotted root.) The herb will also lessen high blood pressure and has a salutary effect on the heart. It is diuretic as well, and an efficient enough painkiller, when nothing stronger is available.

For all these uses, prepare a standard infusion from the leaves and flowers. As figwort is a bitter-tasting herb, the infusion may be sweetened with a little honey.

FOXGLOVE
Digitalis purpurea Family: *Scrophulariaceae*

Found in hedges, ditches and on wooded slopes, foxgloves are a fairly common sight. The thimble-shaped flowers droop from a central

FOXGLOVE *Digitalis purpurea*

stem, their corollas bright purple outside and speckled within. The leaves are downy and finely wrinkled.

Foxglove leaves have a calming effect and are renowned for their regulating effect on the heart. Unfortunately, the correct dosage varies in every case and, as the plant has poisonous properties, its administration is best left to an experienced herbalist. Novices should stick to the *external* use of foxglove leaves: in poultices or compresses these will calm headaches, reduce tumours and lessen inflammation.

FUMITORY
Fumaria officinalis
Family: *Fumariaceae*

Here we have a dainty, fern-like plant, smoky-green in colour and growing in a dense tuft some three to six inches high. From this rises a long thin stem, crowned in summer with clusters of white, mauve or yellow flowers. The leaves are frail and much divided.

Highly esteemed by generations of herbalists, fumitory is a superb liver tonic – as befits a plant 'ruled' by Jupiter. It can be recommended with confidence for all hepatic ailments, from simple biliousness to chronic malfunctioning of the liver. A good digestive herb, it will cure nausea, vomiting and painful

FUMITORY *Fumaria officinalis*

cramps. It is also something of a general pick-me-up, dispelling lassitude and improving concentration.

The whole herb above ground, finely chopped, is traditionally infused in wine. Those who can forgo the wine will find water just as good and cheaper. Prepare a standard infusion and take a cupful daily.

GARLIC
Allium sativum
Family: *Liliaceae*

This familiar plant is not difficult to grow, but non-gardeners can, of course, purchase it from their greengrocer. It is also sold in health food shops in deodorized tablet form.

Garlic is something of a herbal panacea: it relieves rheumatism, clears the chest and improves the lungs – it has long been used to treat tuberculosis. A stout general tonic, it builds up the body's resistance to disease or infection. The brain, the blood, but, alas, not

GARLIC *Allium sativum*

the breath, are improved by its use. Garlic is strongly antiseptic: taken internally it will destroy worms, and used externally will rid the skin of parasites.

Eat the raw cloves and use liberally in cooking. A nineteenth-century manual* gives the following recipe for garlic tablets:

It is also to be taken in the form of pills, with an equal quantity of soap, about four grains of the compound to form one pill, four or five to be taken morning and evening. A few caraway seeds mixed with the composition will take away the offensive smell and taste of garlic.

The writer then goes on to add – 'Reader, if you be troubled with

* Richard Brook, *A New Family Herbal* (Huddersfield, pub. by the author, 1848), p. 104.

asthma, try the above remedy *directly* and be grateful to me for pointing it out.'

GENTIAN *Gentiana campestris*

GENTIAN
Gentiana campestris and others
Family: *Gentianaceae*

There are several varieties of gentian growing both wild and under cultivation, all but one of them remarkable for their intensely blue flowers. (The exception, *Gentiana lutea*, has yellow flowers.) One of the prettiest is Alpine gentian (*Gentiana nivalis*) which thrives best at high altitudes. Gentian is available at herbal stockists and its medicinal derivatives can be obtained from most chemists.

Gentian is said to purify the blood and is an all-round tonic. It stimulates the appetite, calms the digestion, improves the liver and stops biliousness and vomiting. As a strong anti-spasmodic, gentian plays its part in the treatment of various nervous disorders. Years ago, gentian was taken as an antidote to poison, and it can still be used – internally and externally – to treat dangerous bites or stings. The root is the part used for internal treatment: chop fine and make a decoction. For external use prepare a tincture (Gentian Violet) from the root and flowers.

GOLDEN ROD
Solidago virgaurea   Family: *Compositae*
Found on open spaces, heathland and hillsides, especially where there is sandy soil. The lance-shaped leaves of this plant are narrow, slightly toothed and dark green. The upper part of the stem sprouts numerous

short branches each bearing three or four small, daisy-like, bright yellow flowers.

Because of its astringent and antiseptic qualities golden rod has always been valued as a wound herb. Applied externally, the pulped plant (leaves, stalk and flowers, if these are available) will arrest bleeding and prevent infection. It is even believed to halt gangrene and tetanus. Taken internally, the herb reduces high fever and promotes sweating. It is also a fine tonic for the digestion. A specific for jaundice, nausea (including morning sickness) and hay fever, golden rod is also a good general tonic. I have heard it praised also for its dissolvent properties, which lead many herbalists to prescribe it for disorders of the kidneys and bladder.

GOLDEN ROD *Solidago virgaurea*

Prepare a standard infusion from any part of the plant above ground and take a tablespoonful after every meal. Compared with some herbal concoctions, this one tastes quite pleasant.

GOLDEN SEAL

Hydrastia canadensis Family: *Podophyllaceae*

A North American herb with solitary white flowers and red raspberry-like fruit. The powdered root (the part used in medicine) can be purchased from herbal suppliers. Golden seal is worth buying because of its remarkable – some say unique – ability to repair damaged or infected tissue. It is thus an ideal treatment for all internal ulcers and inflammation, however grave, quickly relieving the discomfort to which such conditions give rise.

The same herb also clears up infections of the genital area, and is the only effective treatment for non-specific urethritis.

For internal treatment, add a teaspoonful of powdered root to half a cup of milk and take once daily. Alternatively, mix the powder with a little jam and eat. For external use, add a teaspoonful of root to half a pint of water and use as a lotion.

GROUND IVY
Glechoma hederacea
Family: *Labiatae*

No relation of the true ivy (*Hedera helix*), this trailing plant with its grey, kidney-shaped leaves frequents most hedgerows and woods. In early spring it bears violet-coloured flowers in whorls of two to six.

For centuries, ground ivy has been used to regulate the digestion and to soothe coughs; this little herb is also used in the treatment of ulcers and glandular disorders.

GROUND IVY *Glechoma hederacea*

A strong decongestant, it will remove excess mucus and relieve catarrhal conditions throughout the body. In all cases a standard infusion is made from the flowering plant.

The same herb is believed to have a sedative effect, and was combined with other narcotics in old-fashioned sleeping draughts. In Switzerland the fresh sap (one teaspoonful daily) is held to be a tonic.

HAWTHORN
Crataegus oxycantha
Family: *Rosaceae*

A common hedgerow shrub with dark green leaves and, in spring, frail white blossom, known as 'may'. (In some varieties this blossom may be pink or deep red.) The berries or 'haws' are small, crimson and egg-shaped. Beware of the sharp thorns when harvesting this plant.

HAWTHORN *Crataegus oxycantha*

Of all the cardiac tonics growing wild, few surpass the hawthorn, whose leaves, flowers and berries can be used in a standard infusion, flavoured, if you wish it, with honey. Apart from being a splendid tonic for the heart, hawthorn softens arteries, cures giddiness and reduces palpitations. An infusion of the flowers will also soothe sore throats. Those who dislike botanical infusions,* even sweetened with honey, will be glad to know of hawthorn nectar. This is prepared by packing hawthorn flowers into a wide-necked bottle which is then filled up with brandy. After a month, the brandy should be strained off and stored in a well-corked bottle. Alas, this nectar, though delicious, may not do your heart much good, hawthorn notwithstanding!

HAZEL
Corylus avellana
Family: *Corylaceae*
Country folk maintain that if the season's hazel nuts have thick shells, the winter will be bleak, but if their shells are thin, the chances are the winter will be mild.

Hazel nuts, like hawthorn, are known to improve the heart and prevent hardening of the arteries. But their alleged aphrodisiac virtues† may mean that those with shaky hearts had better stay off them.

HAZEL *Corylus avellana*

HEARTSEASE
Viola tricolor Family: *Violaceae*
Also known as pansy, love-in-idleness and butterfly flower, this

---

* The taking of unpalatable herbs is made easier if the herb is first pounded thoroughly and mixed with cornflour and honey. The resulting paste is then rolled into pellets which, if wrapped in rice paper, can be swallowed with a gulp of water.

† In philtres, they were often combined with cantharides or herbs such as purslane, jasmine, periwinkle and anemone. Readers who find it hard to credit that hazel nuts were ever thought to be aphrodisiac should reflect on the Doctrine of Signatures, according to which endives and carrots were likewise thought once to have erotic properties. For an immoderate passion – due perhaps to over-eating these vegetables – Galen advises a poultice of macerated hemlock.

HEARTSEASE *Viola tricolor*

plant grows wild on heaths, moors and sunny banks. Its flowers are an attractive purple, speckled with white and yellow patches. According to the Doctrine of Signatures, the lower leaves of this herb, being heart shaped, betray its natural sympathy with that organ. Fable has it that the flowers, originally white, were turned purple by one of Cupid's arrows.

Heartsease is a splendid fortifier of the heart. It has other virtues too; it is a strong anti-convulsive and possesses marked sedative properties. Used in the treatment of heart failure, chronic asthma, catarrh and even epilepsy, heartease is the favourite herb of many herbalists. To obtain maximum benefit, a standard infusion should be prepared from the leaves of the plant and a tablespoonful taken two or three times daily, either as a cure or a preventive measure. (Some experts counsel the use of the flowers as well, the purpler the petals the better.) As a lotion this heals sores and other skin ailments.

HEATHER
Family: *Ericaceae*
Heathers flourish on heaths and moorland where the soil is moist and, preferably, peaty. All members of this family have a soothing effect on frayed nerves and revive jaded spirits. They are thus useful herbs to have around when things get you down or when convalescing after illness.

To prepare the herb, make an infusion from well-flowered sprigs and drink a cupful whenever you need it.

HEATHER

HONEYSUCKLE

Lonicera periclymenum   Family: *Caprifoliaceae*

Honeysuckle or woodbine is one of the best-loved wild flowers. As one enthusiastic herbal proclaims, 'Who does not know the Honey-Suckle? which for exquisite beauty and fragrance is an universal favourite. What a lovely sight, to see a trellis before a cottage door covered with Roses, Clematis and Honey-Suckle! although it is no where so beautiful as in its own native places, the borders of woods and in hedges.'

The flowers of this plant, pink, creamy-yellow and purple, are not only pretty but are also medicinal. They are sweet-tasting and may be eaten raw. Alternatively, a delicious syrup may be prepared by infusing four pounds of fresh petals and a quart of boiling water in a covered vessel for twelve hours; express lightly at the end of that time, then decant. Add twice the weight of white sugar and make a syrup. Take a dessert-spoonful daily. Those who would prefer something less sickly – and less fattening – than this, can prepare a standard infusion or else make a decoction from the grated bark (one part bark to seven parts water). Take two cupfuls daily.

Honeysuckle is a grand tonic for the heart and a remedy for most cardiac disorders. It is also good for chest colds, coughs and

HONEYSUCKLE *Lonicera periclymenum*

asthma, rheumatism and arthritis, liver trouble, sore throat, dropsy and ailments of the skin. I first tried some at the age of twelve when suffering from mumps and I have since prescribed it in all cases of glandular disturbance. Here, infusions of the bark are best and, if appropriate, the leaves can be used externally to help reduce any obvious swelling.

HOREHOUND *Marrubium vulgare*

HOREHOUND
Marrubium vulgare
Family: *Labiatae*
Found in pastures and wastes, this herb has oval tooth-edged leaves and, where they join the stalk, clusters of tiny white flowers. The Egyptians called this plant the 'seed of Horus'.

Older herbals, like the *Hortulus* of Strabo of Swabia (807–49), recommend horehound tea for all 'pulmonary afflictions', and it is certainly a useful winter stand-by when coughs and colds are common. According to Culpeper, 'a syrup made of horehound . . . is very good for old coughs to rid phlegm; as also to void cold rheums from the lungs of old people, and also for those that are asthmatic or short winded.' This herb is also mildly laxative, diuretic and a vermifuge. The leaves should be infused and their flavour improved by sweetening. One sherry-glassful daily is usually sufficient.

In Wales an infusion of the chopped herb is used externally and internally to cure eczema and shingles.

HORSE RADISH
Cochlearia armoracia
Family: *Cruciferae*
Mostly cultivated, but frequenting waste places as well, this plant has large oblong leaves and small whitish flowers. More important for both culinary (horse radish sauce) and medicinal purposes is the root, which has a biting hot taste.

Horse radish is used to treat disorders of the renal system and will generally cure related dropsical conditions. It is believed

HORSE RADISH *Cochlearia armoracia*

also to reduce internal growths and tumours. Take a teaspoonful of the grated root every morning or, if this burns your tongue, spread it thinly on a buttered crust and eat.

As a poultice herb, chopped horse radish is antiseptic, relieves local discomfort and encourages healing.

HORSETAIL
Equisetum arvense Family: *Equisetaceae*
A common plant, often found in damp soil (meadows, marshes etc.). It has a yellowish-green stalk, girt at intervals with whorls of small green 'branches'. Not a very pretty plant.

Horsetail can be used to check haemorrhages, diarrhoea and the retention of excess fluid. The same standard infusion, made from the chopped stem, has a tonic effect on the liver and kidneys. It will also heal both internal and external ulcers.

In the bath water, horsetail will soothe pain and, as a lotion, will prompt the rapid healing of sores, wounds, shingles, etc. Added to a bowl of boiling water, its vapours will help clear stuffy tubes in the nose and chest. Finally, an essential oil rubbed nightly on weak, brittle fingernails will improve their condition.

HOUNDSTONGUE
Cynoglossum officinale
Family: *Boraginaceae*

Houndstongue may be sought along roadsides and on waste land, where it can be recognized by its lance-like leaves and clusters of dullish-crimson, bell-shaped flowers. The flowering stalk grows to a height of about thirty inches and the plant has a slightly musty smell.

Coughs and catarrh, even chronic bronchitis, are success-fully treated with this herb when drunk in a standard infusion which may be sweetened with

HOUNDSTONGUE *Cynoglossum officinale*

117

sugar or honey. The dosage, one tablespoonful daily, should not be exceeded as the plant has marked narcotic tendencies. Applied externally, it reduces tumours, boils and goitres, and will soothe most bruises and scratches.

HOUSELEEK
Sempervivum tectorum   Family: *Crassulaceae*
Once common everywhere on garden walls and on the roofs of buildings, houseleek is now sold as a pot or rockery plant by horticulturists. Houseleeks traditionally come under the patronage of Jupiter (though in magic they belong to Venus) and were formerly known as Jove's Beard (*Jovis Barba*). So strong was the belief in their ability to deflect lightning that Charlemagne ordered that every dwelling in his empire should have them on its roof.

These succulent plants yield a juice much used by herbalists as eye- and ear-drops. It may also be applied locally to bruises and ulcers or as a cure for warts, erysipelas and ringworm. The flowers were once thought to be unlucky and were usually cut off before they could bloom. The Greeks regarded houseleek, known as *Strorgethron*, as a powerful love philtre.

HYSSOP
Hyssopus officinalis   Family: *Labiatae*
Growing wild in warm countries and frequently cultivated elsewhere, this aromatic plant has long lanceolate leaves and clusters of light blue flowers.

Hyssop, a cleansing herb, relieves catarrh and reduces the secretion of mucus. It also regulates blood pressure (high or low), clears the chest and calms the nerves. As it promotes sweating, this herb is useful when coping with fevered patients. It also improves the digestion and protects the body from infection.

Prepare a standard infusion of the leaves and diced stem. As a lotion, this brew relieves inflammation and bruising, being noteworthy for its beneficial effect on black eyes!

IVY
Hedera helix   Family: *Araliaceae*
In woods and along walls, the ivy is our commonest evergreen climber.

HOUSELEEK *Sempervivum tectorum*   IVY *Hedera helix*

Its long, trailing stems and five-lobed leaves will be familiar to everyone.

Readers are warned that only a small quantity of this herb should be used. In the right amount it will reduce swollen glands, calm fevers and cure dropsy, the right amount being five leaves infused in half a pint of water. The correct dosage is one tablespoonful taken three times daily. Externally, an ointment containing the pulped leaf soothes stiff joints and aching muscles.

KNAPWEED

Centaurea nigra   Family: *Compositae*

Knapweed is an unprickly member of the thistle family, and has narrow, greyish leaves and purple, slightly scented flowers. Young girls once wore knapweed underneath their bodice, believing it would flower should they chance to meet their future spouse.

This herb is of immense value in the treatment of glandular disorders. (For immediate local relief, prepare a hot poultice.) It also relieves catarrh, especially when mixed with speedwell, and revives the appetite, particularly during lengthy periods of convalescence. In all cases, prepare an infusion of the flowers or a decoction of the bruised root. Some enthusiasts eat the fresh flowers.

The larger knapweed (*Centaurea scabiosa*) has the same virtues. It is distinguishable by its brighter flowers and bigger size.

LAVENDER

LAVENDER
Family: *Lavandulae* (*Labiatae*)

Thanks to its pleasing fragrance, lavender has been much cultivated since very early times. The name itself (from the Latin, *lavare*, to wash) refers to the Roman custom of scenting bath water with the leaves and flowers of this delightful aromatic.

Long used as a nerve tonic, cough cure and anti-paralytic, lavender is also renowned, when used as a gargle or mouth-wash, for its ability to improve the gums and check halitosis. For all these uses, prepare a standard infusion of flowering sprigs. An essential oil of lavender, for external application, soothes headaches, reduces inflammation and calms angry joints and muscles.

A fine nerve tonic may be had by preparing a tincture (*Lavandulae composita*) of lavender, rosemary, crushed cinnamon and nutmeg. Dabbed on the forehead, this eases nervous headaches and quickly calms a fever.

LILY-OF-THE-VALLEY
Convallaria majalis
Family: *Liliaceae*

Widely cultivated, but still found wild in some woodlands, this pretty plant is a formidable brain, lymph and heart herb, from which the drug convallotoxin is obtained. Lily-of-the-Valley has been successfully employed in treating patients recovering from strokes, especially when their speech is slow to return. It also soothes the nerves, reduces high blood pressure and cures various forms of

LILY-OF-THE-VALLEY *Convallaria majalis*

dropsy. Prepare an infusion from the flowering stalks (half an ounce to every pint of water). The dosage in all cases is four tablespoonfuls daily.

LIME *Tilia europaea*

LIME (*in U.S.*, LINDEN)
Tilia europaea
Family: *Tiliaceae*

Lime flowers provide us with one of the most popular of all herbal teas. Though its overall effect is tonic, and therefore mildly stimulating, this drink calms the nerves and ensures restful sleep. It also relieves feverish conditions and has a sedative effect on the chest, halting dry, stubborn coughs.

An infusion of lime flowers, used as a lotion, will condition the hair and scalp. An essential oil may also be prepared for more occasional use.

LOOSESTRIFE
Lythrum salicaria
Family: *Lythraceae*

Loosestrife grows along the banks of streams and rivers. It has tall, lance-like leaves and mauve flowers that appear from mid- to late summer. The plant often reaches a height of five feet. According to Culpeper, this herb was one of the best he could recommend for the sight, and it is still used, often in the company of eyebright, as an eye lotion. Use half an ounce of herb to half a pint of boiling, slightly saline water. Steep for thirty minutes, strain and use.

LOOSESTRIFE *Lythrum salicaria*

LUCERNE
Medicago sativa   Family: *Papilionaceae*
Known too as alfalfa, this fodder plant is widely cultivated. It has
small greyish-green leaves and tiny white or purple flowers. The
benefits that herbivores derive from this mineral-rich plant are
available to humans as well. Primarily a tonic and restorer of energy,
it also improves the kidneys and, by its alkalizing action, neutralizes
acid indigestion. It is a fine herb for those who are physically active,
and so for all athletes and sportsmen.

The plant may be eaten in salads or else a tisane prepared from the
fresh or dried herb.

LUCERNE *Medicago sativa*

MAIDENHAIR FERN *Adiantum capillus-veneris*

MAIDENHAIR FERN
Adiantum capillus-veneris   Family: *Filices*
A cherished occupant of Victorian drawing-rooms, this plant can
still be bought quite cheaply. Cheaper still is the dried herb, obtainable
from most herbalist suppliers.

The leaves of this fern have a therapeutic effect on the heart and
lungs. The leaves may be eaten raw, or in a standard infusion which
may also be used as a scalp lotion to improve the hair and stop premature
baldness.

MARIGOLD
Calendula officinalis
Family: *Compositae*

The orange marigold is a prolific garden plant, but readers without gardens can buy dried flowerheads quite cheaply. Such is this flower's feeling for the sun that it opens its petals at nine and closes them at four – hence its other name, solsequia.

A disinfectant herb, marigold has been used in the effective treatment of ulcers (internal and external) and open sores. Its sustained use will also relieve catarrh. The flowers may be eaten raw, taken as a standard

MARIGOLD *Calendula officinalis*

infusion or the latter applied as a lotion. The same plant cures varicose veins and other circulatory troubles.

As a lotion, a marigold infusion (petals only) provides the ideal balancer of an over-oily skin and all complexions will benefit from a salve or ointment composed of this flower.

MARSHMALLOW *Althaea officinalis*

MARSHMALLOW
Althaea officinalis
Family: *Malvaceae*

Found on waste land generally, but on the coast especially, this herb has thick downy leaves and pretty mauvish flowers which appear in clusters at the height of summer.

Marshmallow is one of the best herbal cough remedies and is used to treat most pectoral disorders, including pleurisy. It will also release retained afterbirth. In all cases prepare a standard infusion or a decoction from several finely diced roots. Either preparation, applied externally, will reduce inflammation, and the decoction is said to relieve soreness in the breasts.

MEADOW SAFFRON
Colchicum autumnale
Family: *Liliaceae*

A plant that favours moist places, its sad message in one version of the language of flowers is 'My best days are over'. Meadow saffron has large, oblong leaves and, in autumn, purple crocus-like flowers.

The botanical name of this plant recalls its connection with Colchis, where the great witch Medea practised her herbal enchantments. Nowadays, the herb is used to alleviate muscular aches and pains. (Prepare a standard infusion/decoction for external use.) It was once a much-vaunted cure for gout.

MEADOW SAFFRON *Colchicum autumnale*

MEADOWSWEET
Spiraea ulmaria Family: *Rosaceae*

Meadowsweet grows freely in damp meadows and on the banks of streams and rivers. Its sweetness comes from its tiny white flowers that crown the top of each stem in dense scented clusters. This plant flowers in the summer months and attains a height of two to three feet. So fond was Elizabeth I of this herb that the floors of her apartments were always strewn with it.

The only medicinal use of meadowsweet with which I am familiar is to settle an upset stomach. All cases of enteritis and diarrhoea respond to its action. Prepare an infusion using one ounce of herb to three-quarters of a pint of boiling water. A tea-cup of the beverage – which is very rich in iron and magnesium – should be taken as required. Some herbalists recommend meadowsweet for the treatment of high blood pressure, diabetes and disorders of the blood.

Meadowsweet beer is a pleasing and refreshing drink. It is prepared from equal quantities of meadowsweet, dandelion and agrimony which are boiled together for twenty minutes in double the quantity of water. Add two pounds of sugar to each gallon of strained liquid together with half an ounce of yeast and the juice of a lemon. Leave the mixture to ferment and bottle later.

MIGNONETTE

Reseda lutea Family: *Resedaceae*
Wild mignonette thrives on chalky soil and is frequently found along roads and railway embankments. Its central stem supports a few sparse leaves and numerous tiny flowers, greenish white and sweetly scented.

This little plant is a gentle narcotic and so makes a dependable nightcap when stress or worry promise you a sleepless night. An efficient painkiller, mignonette calms headaches and soothes frayed nerves. A standard infusion is customary and this may also be used as a soothing lotion.

MEADOWSWEET *Spiraea ulmaria*

MIGNONETTE *Reseda lutea*. The ripe seed vessel

MINT
Mentha viridis
Family: *Labiatae*

Wild mint is said to favour shady, damp places, but I have found it on dry, rocky ground as well. The cultivated varieties are no less beneficial than the wild. Among the ancients, the scent of this herb was highly esteemed – the philosopher Seneca, though a Stoic, died in a bath strewn with mint. The herb's culinary virtues were also known in classical times: Pliny says that 'the very smell of mint restores and revives the spirit just as its taste excites the appetite.' Mint's ability to prevent milk from curdling was also known.

MINT *Mentha viridis*

In herbalism, mint tea is used to help the digestion, revive the appetite and alleviate rheumatism. The Arabs have always believed that mint increases virility, and some modern herbalists still prescribe it in cases of impotence and decreased libido.

Peppermint (*Mentha piperita*) and spearmint (*Mentha spicata*) are likewise used in herbalism to improve the appetite and digestion. They quicken the circulation and can be used to treat anaemia – but the cause of the anaemia must be identified before a complete cure can be essayed. Added to the bathwater, an infusion of peppermint helps cure skin disorders and invigorates the bather.

MISTLETOE
Viscum album   Family: *Loranthaceae*

An evergreen semi-parasitic plant that grows on other trees, most commonly the poplar and the apple. It bears small yellow flowers in early spring, but better known are its pearly berries. Mistletoe (the 'Golden Bough') was chief of the seven sacred herbs of the Druids, the others being vervain, henbane, primrose, pulsatilla, clover and

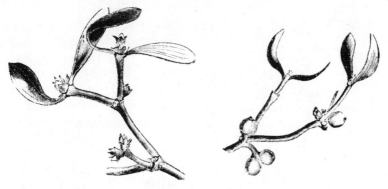

MISTLETOE *Viscum album*

wolf's-bane. Readers keen to follow the Druidic example should gather their mistletoe on the sixth day of the moon's waning. (For more elaborate ritual details, see Pliny's *Natural History*, VI, 249.)

In olden times mistletoe was the accepted treatment for dropsy and epilepsy, although nowadays its commonest use is to strengthen the nerves and improve the circulation. A good heart tonic and anti-sclerotic, it also reduces high blood pressure. Prepare an infusion of the leaves and young branches (diced), using two ounces of herb to half a pint of water. It is unnecessary in the case of this plant to allow it to steep for more than thirty minutes. The dosage is one tablespoonful daily, increasing to three if no improvement is shown. Rudolf Steiner praised this herb's therapeutic virtues, although many herbalists advise against giving it to children.

The juice from mistletoe berries has its uses as well. Obstinate pimples will disappear if dabbed with the juice, and it will also loosen stiff joints when massaged into the skin.

MULLEIN
Verbascum thapsus   Family: *Scrophulariaceae*
A frequenter of roadsides and dry, sunny wastes, mullein has wide, grey-green leaves covered with a thick woolly down. The flowers, borne aloft on long spikes, are yellow and numerous.

Something of a herbal cure-all, mullein is employed in herbalism for a wide variety of ailments. It is, for instance, a versatile chest herb, used to treat everything from asthma to pneumonia, pleurisy to

MULLEIN *Verbascum thapsus*

whooping cough. It is astringent, also, and is commonly prescribed for bleeding in any part of the body, for catarrh and excess mucus. In addition, this plant is a general pain-reliever, and, being sedative, induces sleep.

Prepare a standard infusion of the leaves and flowers (if available). The same brew can also be used as an inhalation to clear the chest and nasal passages. (Sufferers from asthma and hay fever vastly benefit from this treatment.) As a lotion, it provides a soothing gargle whose analgesic effect is particularly welcome when the tonsils are inflamed.

NASTURTIUM
Tropaeolum
Family: *Tropaeolaceae*

A familiar garden plant, easily recognized by its thin, flat leaves which are veined and bright green. The flowers are a vivid blaze of orange, red and yellow.

Nasturtium leaves, a tasty addition to every green salad, are strongly antiseptic. As an internal cleanser, this plant is of special benefit to the blood and the digestive system. I know several herbalists who praise it also for its tonic effect on the nervous system, and at least one claims it will improve the sight.

NASTURTIUM *Tropaeolaceae*

NETTLE
Urtica dioica
Family: *Urticaceae*

On waste land, pastures and in hedges, nettles will be found in plenty. They are a most potent herb, their many qualities compensating for the stung fingers that inevitably accompany their harvest. (The sting, caused by the formic acid in the plant, can be soothed by rubbing the spot with dock leaves (*Rumex obtusifolus*). You will find that Providence generally plants these leaves alongside nettle beds.)

The nettle is widely used to treat rheumatism and poor circulation, but it also cures bronchitis, reduces the risk of haemorrhages and dispels melancholia. For all these purposes, the leaves may be boiled and then eaten like any green vegetable, or else used for an infusion. A decoction may also be made from the root, this being particularly good at dissolving renal stones and other internal obstructions.

NETTLE *Urtica dioica*

Pulped nettle leaves make a marvellous compress and bring cooling relief when inflammation is present.

OAK
Quercus robur, and others   Family: *Fagaceae*

The young bark, leaves and, less often, the acorns* of this tree are valued by herbalists for their ability to staunch bleeding. A standard

---

* The acorns were once believed to cure drunkenness, and a distilled spirit from them (*Spiritus Glandium Quercus*) was prescribed as a cure for alcoholism. Pliny advocates a cabbage leaf as a safeguard against intemperance and, strangely enough, a substance extracted from cabbage is now used to treat dipsomania.

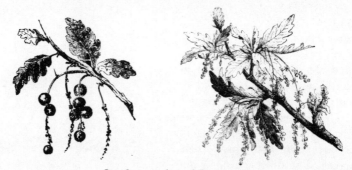

OAK *Quercus robur* and *Quercus cerris*

infusion of the leaves or a decoction of the macerated bark will serve as a safeguard against internal haemorrhaging and will check over-copious menstruation. The same treatment will heal damaged tissue in the stomach and intestines.

Oak leaves in the bath are both deodorant and relaxing. They soothe inflammation and can be trusted as a *toilette de Venus*.

PARSLEY
Petroselinum sativum   Family: *Umbelliferae*
A widely cultivated seasoning plant, parsley has a tonic effect on the entire urinary system. For this purpose, parsley tablets may be bought, although the fresh herb is probably better. (It purifies the breath as well.) All disorders of the bladder and kidneys respond well to treatment with this plant, as do rheumatism, sciatica and jaundice. Some herbalists recommend parsley for treating cancer, a condition which, according to them, it also helps to prevent.

A tisane can be made from the dried herb when the fresh is unavailable.

PERIWINKLE
Vinca major/minor   Family: *Apocynaceae*
Periwinkle grows in woods and on banks where its pale blue flowers contrast with the dark evergreen of its leaves. This herb is dear to Venus, it being said that if two lovers eat a sprig of it together, they will stay in love all their lives.

Periwinkle is a natural tonic and a specific for the treatment of an upset digestion (diarrhoea, flatulence, etc.). Ulcers of the throat and mouth, diphtheria, diabetes and disorders of the skin and scalp, all are conditions for which peri- winkle is traditionally prescribed. A standard infusion can be used for internal or external treatment, as appropriate.

From several of the plants of the *Vinca* family is obtained the drug vinblastine sulphate, now being tested in America for the treatment of Hodgkins' disease.

PERIWINKLE *Vinca minor*

PIMPERNEL
Anagallis arvensis Family: *Primulaceae*
This little plant makes its home almost everywhere, and generously flowers from spring to late autumn. The pimpernel has small oval-shaped leaves and long slender stalks, each bearing a bright scarlet flower. For country people these flowers are a useful barometer, for they close whenever rain threatens.

The ancient Greeks were particularly fond of this herb, which

PIMPERNEL *Anagallis arvensis*

they used in the treatment of eye diseases. (The pimpernel's habit of closing its petals at dusk may first have suggested a connection with the eyes.) The herb is also prescribed in cases of jaundice, dropsy and inflammation. The plant has cosmetic properties, too; applied as a skin lotion, a standard infusion regulates the pigmentation, removing freckles and other minor blemishes. The same lotion is rumoured to act as a hair restorer, but even if that rumour turns out to be false, the herb will offer comfort, for it dispels melancholia.

PLANTAIN
Plantago lanceolata
Family: *Plantaginaceae*

Plantain seems to flourish almost everywhere – tradition maintains that it springs up wherever English people set foot, no matter what the climate. It has narrow, lance-like leaves, and stalks that end in small brown spikes. From these grow minute white flowers.

PLANTAIN *Plantago lanceolata*

Plantain leaves are used to cure bronchitis, asthma and all respiratory afflictions. The same standard infusion also assists the digestion. The leaves may be applied raw to stings and wounds that are slow to heal, or used as a poultice to combat inflammation.

POPPY (RED)
Papaver rhoeas
Family: *Papaveraceae*

The common red poppy, though unwelcomed by the farmer, adds a pleasant touch of scarlet to our cornfields. (In classical mythology this plant was sacred to Ceres.) Its crepe-like flowers appear from late spring onwards and are followed by the distinctive poppy head in which the seeds are stored. The milky juice obtained from this has narcotic properties, though less so than the white poppy from which opium is obtained.

RED POPPY *Papaver rhoeas*

The red poppy is not among the plants most commonly used by modern herbalists, but its leaves do have definite tonic virtues. In parts of the West Country both leaves and petals are valued for their soothing effect (in a standard infusion) on sore throats and chests. They are also used to treat catarrh, hay fever, asthma and other respiratory complaints. A few crushed poppy heads added to a linseed poultice ($\frac{1}{4}$ lb. linseed, $\frac{1}{2}$ oz. olive oil, both well stirred in one pint of boiling water) will reduce pain and swelling.

PRIMROSE
Primula vulgaris
Family: *Primulaceae*

Primroses still grow wild throughout the countryside. Their flowers, the palest of yellow, are borne on pinkish stalks that emerge from clumps of soft, wrinkled leaves, their undersides thickly veined.

Like its cousin, the cowslip, the primrose is mildly narcotic, and, as a result, offers a safe, non-addictive cure for insomnia. (It also alleviates rheumatism and arthritis.) The leaves and flowers may be eaten raw, but more palatable is an infusion taken before going to bed.

PRIMROSE *Primula vulgaris*

RASPBERRY
Rubus idaeus   Family: *Rosaceae*

The raspberry grows wild in woods and sheltered heathland but is also widely cultivated. It is best known as a gynaecic herb, thanks to its proven worth in curing illnesses peculiar to women. These include – to name but a few – frigidity, uterine disorders, menstrual discomfort and threatened abortion. It is also a sound tonic both during and after pregnancy, as well as helping women through the menopause. (Prepare a raspberry leaf tea and drink several strong cupfuls daily for all the above conditions. The fruit, when available, should also be eaten.)

Apart from these special uses, raspberries themselves are a good mineral-rich restorative and have a kindly effect on the nerves.

RASPBERRY *Rubus idaeus*

Because of this plant's link with the reproductive system, the leaves have acquired the reputation of being aphrodisiac.

RED CLOVER *Trifolium pratense*

RED CLOVER
Trifolium pratense
Family: *Papilionaceae*
The red or purple clover grows wild in pastures, meadows and at roadsides. It is also cultivated for fodder. The dense purple flower-heads appear in spring and can still be seen in early autumn. In the language of flowers, the clover's message lies in its leaves: three, the usual number, signify eternity; four, perfect balance; five portend fame; six, money; and seven, life-long prosperity. A four-leaved clover has the additional virtue of dissolving fairy spells and enabling its owner to spurn spurious glamour. There is also a belief that four grains of

wheat wrapped inside a clover leaf enables one to see elves and goblins.

The flowers of the red clover are important in herbalism because they are believed to prevent cancer. Many authorities assert that they will even arrest the progress of existing growths. Apart from this, they are traditionally used in the treatment of headache, neuralgia, nausea, gastric trouble, ulcers and most glandular ailments.

The flower-heads should be eaten raw (about a dozen daily), or dried and made into a standard infusion.

REED (Common Reed)
Arundo phragmites, and others
Family: *Gramineae*

Common everywhere in marshes, fens and along the edges of pools, reeds grow to a height of over seven feet, rather less in exposed places.

At home in Wales the white pith inside reeds was regarded as a cure for goitre. It was carefully extracted and two or three tea-spoonfuls swallowed daily. Apart from its possible effect on the thyroid gland, it is most certainly a good lymph tonic. This inner pith (same dosage) is used also to treat ailments of the urino-genital tract.

Externally, pulped reeds offer a cool, refreshing compress.

REED *Arundo donax*

ROSE (WILD)
Rosa canina, and others   Family: *Rosaceae*

These, the most charming of all roses, grow in copses and hedgerows, their flowering period extending from spring to the middle of summer. The pink or white flowers are fragrantly scented and the hips that replace them are one of the richest natural sources of vitamin C.

The fresh or dried flowers are used to prepare an infusion which

WILD ROSE *Rosa gallica*

fortifies the heart and brain. (Even garden roses are good for this, especially the white varieties.) Catarrh, female ailments and stomach disorders are but a few of the other conditions for which this plant is prescribed.

ROSEMARY
Rosmarinus officinalis   Family: *Labiatae*

Rosemary was once widely cultivated and is still a popular garden plant, with its spiky dark green leaves and distinctive scent. We know that in the sixth century Charlemagne decreed that it should be grown in all the imperial gardens (where the chief gardener was an Englishman named Alcuin), and it was beloved of the Romans long before that.

As a medicine, rosemary provides a valuable heart and liver tonic and also helps reduce high blood pressure. It is widely used too in the treatment of 'nerves', digestive disorders and menstrual pains. In all cases a small cupful of the standard infusion should be taken each morning on rising. Other uses of the herb set down in the thirteenth-century Myddfai manuscript are these:

> If the leaves be put beneath your pillow, you will be well pro-
> tected from troublesome dreams and all mental anxiety. Used
> as a lotion, this herb or its oil will cure all pains in the head,
> and a spoonful of the herb mixed with honey and melted butter
> cannot help but cure your coughing.

Rosemary is, of course, well known as a fine tonic for the scalp and skin. It adds lustre to the hair and is a common ingredient of many commercial shampoos. Rosemary and distilled water were the constituents of Hungary Water, a rejuvenating lotion named after Queen Elizabeth of Hungary, whose use of it kept her skin free from wrinkles. The good doctors of Myddfai counselled the use of this plant for the same purpose:

> A fine thing it is to boil in water the leaves and flowers and to use the mixture as a face wash. Do not wipe the face afterwards, but let it dry naturally. The truth is that by regularly washing their faces in this way the wise will keep their youth until the day they die.

RUE *Ruta graveolens*

RUE
Ruta graveolens
Family: *Rutaceae*
Rue is widely cultivated. It has flat, grey-green leaves and small greeny-yellow flowers; its most noticeable characteristics are its pungent smell and bitter taste.

Rue has been called the 'herb of grace' because its bitterness makes it the symbol of repentance (cf. *Richard II*, III, iv); it was much used, with St John's wort, by witch-finders and exorcists in the sixteenth century. Among the Muslims it is highly revered, for it was blessed by the grateful Prophet after it had cured him of an illness.

A very potent herb, and one that needs to be taken quite sparingly, it cures many mental disorders. It improves the condition of the veins and arteries and will cure cramp. It is also expert at relieving sciatica and many forms of rheumatism. A teaspoonful of leaves infused in three-quarters of a pint of water is ample. Take a dessertspoonful nightly before retiring to bed, but suspend the treatment if, as

137

occasionally happens, you find that the herb upsets your stomach.

Rue's active principle, rutin, is frequently used in naturopathy, and rutin tea is obtainable at most health food shops. It is a respected tonic for the nerves, the glands and the arteries. It also reduces high blood pressure.

Sage
Salvia officinalis
Family: *Labiatae*
An aromatic, sun-loving plant with grey-green leaves and mauvish flowers, sage is widely cultivated for culinary use. Apart from its value in cooking, it is used to treat coughs, colds, headaches and fevers. It is also good for the liver, bile and the whole digestive system. A standard infusion of the leaves and young sprigs used as a gargle or mouthwash will cure sore throats and gums, and, as a lotion, will heal

SAGE *Salvia officinalis*

ulcers, sores and other skin eruptions. (It will also staunch bleeding from wounds.) Sage has always been thought of as good for the brain, improving the memory and, in some cases, even as a cure for insanity. It is also powerfully nervine and will stop any involuntary trembling of the limbs. Finally, a sprig of sage in the wardrobe will keep away moths.

St John's Wort (Perforated variety)
Hypericum perforatum   Family: *Hypericaceae*
This plant has a pale brown stem, branched at the top, and oblong stalkless leaves growing in pairs. On these are transparent spots (oil glands), which on the unperforated varieties are rust-coloured and were believed by pious country folk to mark the blood of St John the Baptist. The flowers are bright yellow and appear in late summer. This herb has long been linked with magic, and its ancient name *Fuga Daemonum* testifies to its alleged ability to repel demons.

St John's wort works on the central nervous system and for years has been a popular cure for neuritis. Because of its painkilling properties, it used once to be given to patients recovering from operations. (It prevented haemorrhages as well.) In all cases, prepare a standard infusion from the leaves and chopped stem. Used externally, this lotion heals scalds, blisters and all minor wounds, while an oil incorporating the herb has been used since classical times both as a soothing rub and as a dressing for wounds slow to heal.

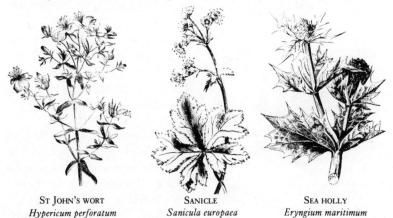

ST JOHN'S WORT
Hypericum perforatum

SANICLE
Sanicula europaea

SEA HOLLY
Eryngium maritimum

SANICLE
Sanicula europaea Family: *Umbelliferae*
A shade-loving plant to be found in woods and among dense bushes. Its flowers are white or pinkish-red in colour, somewhat sparse and borne in umbels.

The whole plant, flowers, leaves and root, may be used to treat catarrhal conditions and inflammation. Prepare a standard infusion from the flowering plant, or a decoction from the root, either being suitable for internal or external use (nasal douches or direct application to wounds and swellings).

SEA HOLLY
Eryngium maritimum Family: *Umbelliferae*
This herb frequents sea coasts, and has tough, spiky leaves of a pearly-grey colour. The flowers are blue and mildly scented. Like most plants with fragrant blue flowers (cf. lavender and violet), sea holly is

good for the nerves. A standard infusion should be made from the chopped leaves which, apart from being a mineral-rich tonic, are used to treat various disorders of the liver and endocrine glands. They are also gently aperient.

The decocted root of this plant, known as Eryngo, was once a favourite sweetmeat. It is still popular in the Middle East.

SEAKALE *Crambe maritima*

SEAKALE
Crambe maritima
Family: *Cruciferae*
Common on sea cliffs and shores, this plant has broad cabbage-like leaves and white flowers. The latter are preceded by purplish sprouts, much esteemed by eighteenth-century gourmets.

This mineral-rich herb will fight a curious assortment of ills, including general debility, constipation, dental decay, rheumatism and urinary disorders. A few shredded leaves should be eaten raw in salads or else used to make the customary brew. (As this plant is slightly laxative, some discretion is required when taking it.)

Externally, the infusion provides a useful mouth-wash which strengthens the gums, heals ulcers and combats oral infection.

SEA LAVENDER
Statice limonium   Family: *Plumbaginaceae*
Common enough in muddy salt marshes along the coast, sea lavender has thin, pointed leaves which grow from the root and are brittle to the touch. The flowers have a similar parchment-like texture and are borne in corymbs at the end of leafless stalks. As the name suggests, these flowers are pale lavender in colour.

This herb is cooling, and thus of value during fevers. It also arrests bleeding, prevents haemorrhages and, as it halts diarrhoea, is a useful stand-by when treating dysentery or enteritis. A wound herb, it encourages the rapid healing of damaged tissue.

For internal use, prepare a standard infusion from the flowering sprigs. Externally, apply the pulped flowers direct to wounds and injuries.

SKULLCAP *Scutellaria galericulata*

SKULLCAP
Scutellaria galericulata
Family: *Labiatae*
Moist meadows and riversides are the usual haunt of skullcap. It has oblong, pointed leaves and large downy flowers, which grow in pairs between the leaves and stem. These flowers are a vivid blue, this colour, as we have already noted, being typical of many of the best nerve herbs.

Here we have one of my favourite herbs, and one deserving closer scrutiny by orthodox medicine. No other plant has, to my knowledge, a more beneficial effect on the nervous system. Because of its sedative properties, skullcap is superb for treating nervous tension, over-excitement and even insanity. It rarely fails to defeat insomnia when that condition springs from an over-active mind. An anti-spasmodic, skullcap is used to treat epilepsy, convulsions, chorea and any involuntary trembling of the limbs. It will also allay the more distressing consequences of withdrawal from an addiction to drugs or alcohol.

All parts of the plant above ground can be employed. Prepare a standard infusion and take a mugful night and morning.

Skullcap is one of the herbs traditionally held to cure infertility.

SNOWDROP
Galanthus nivalis   Family: *Amaryllidaceae*
The straight narrow leaves of the snowdrop are one of the first signs that nature has survived the harsh cold of winter. Soon the leaves are followed by the flower itself, three sepals of purest white and three petals of white tinged with green. Tradition has it that Druids planted

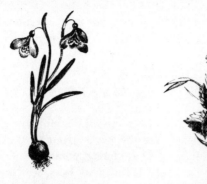

SNOWDROP *Galanthus nivalis*   SPEEDWELL *Veronica officinalis*

snowdrops in their sacred groves. The snowdrop has a short day; the flower opens at ten and shuts again at four.

Appropriately enough, the snowdrop offers help in dealing with discomforts occasioned by the cold, being a reliable cure for frostbite and chilblains. An ointment should be prepared using the crushed bulbs of the plant.

Ophthalmological specialists now use an extract from these bulbs in the treatment of glaucoma.

SORREL

Rumex acetosa   Family: *Polygonaceae*

Growing abundantly in meadows and pastures, this member of the dock family has long-stalked, arrow-shaped leaves which have a sour taste – hence the name sorrel (see p. 80). The reddish flowers grow in whorls, the male on one plant, female on another.

Sorrel leaves are a good refrigerant and are beneficial to the blood. They can be used to treat jaundice, liver complaints and most disorders of the renal system (they are strongly dissolvent). Internal ulcers also respond to the same treatment. Prepare a standard infusion.

As a lotion, this infusion will heal boils, abscesses and sores, while a poultice from the leaves reduces inflammation.

SPEEDWELL

Veronica officinalis   Family: *Scrophulariaceae*

Speedwell (or veronica) is a tiny trailing plant with oval leaves and pale-blue flowers, an inhabitant of clearings, fields and hedgerows.

Herbalists prescribe the flowering plant in cases of catarrh, bronchitis, asthma and digestive trouble. It is also used to treat most skin eruptions, such as sores, ulcers, pimples, but is particularly recommended for eczema and pruritis. In all cases, prepare a standard infusion for internal or external treatment, as appropriate. The same infusion can also be applied as an eye lotion for the treatment of conjunctivitis and kindred disorders. It is reputed to improve the vision.

STINKING IRIS *Iris foetidissima*

STINKING IRIS
Iris foetidissima
Family: *Iridaceae*
This plant's name describes it perfectly. A member of the iris family, it has stiff, sword-like leaves and dull, mauve flowers, darkly veined. If bruised, the plant gives off an unpleasant smell. Unlike other irises, which tend to prefer moist soil, this one fares best on dry, calcareous soil and is often found in woodland clearings.

I value this herb, since its root provides a strong, natural painkiller which is one of the few remedies for migraine. I use it to treat a miscellany of aches and pains, both muscular and nervous. This plant is anti-spasmodic and was once the standard herbal treatment for epilepsy and hysteria.

Prepare a weak decoction of the diced root and take a tablespoonful up to three times daily. Because the root is also laxative, this dosage may need to be reduced.

STRAWBERRY
Fragaria vesca   Family: *Rosaceae*
Both the wild and garden varieties possess considerable medicinal value. Strawberries themselves are remarkably cooling: their consumption with cream on a hot summer's day is thus more than self-indulgence.

For fevers and excessive perspiration, a tisane of strawberry

STRAWBERRY *Fragaria vesca*

leaves can scarcely be bettered. The plant is also astringent, and thus useful in dealing with diarrhoea, over-copious menstruation, threatened abortion, and any risk of haemorrhage. For these purposes, prepare a standard infusion, which is also a fine regulator of the liver and digestive system. Among older herbalists, there persists a belief that strawberry leaves – possibly because of their iron content – will cure anaemia and have a tonic effect on the blood. As for the fruit itself, this is held to fortify the nerves.

The cosmetic virtues of strawberry juice have been noted elsewhere. The juice can also be used to treat more serious skin ailments (eczema, pruritis, etc.). An infusion of the leaves, used as a lotion, works equally well, and, I have discovered, is particularly good at curing styes. Finally, teeth that have become discoloured or encrusted with tartar can be cleaned with strawberry juice.

SUNDEW
Drosera rotundifolia
Family: *Droseraceae*

As its botanical name implies, the leaves of this plant are round. They are also covered with red hairs. More characteristic still are the viscid drops they secrete, which glisten in the sun like dew and give the plant its name. All species of sundew are insectiverous, and the Australian varieties have quite voracious appetites.

SUNDEW *Drosera rotundifolia*

Known in America as the 'old folk's herb', sundew has a beneficial effect on the respiratory system, and is a good treatment for those dry coughs to which the elderly are often prone. It also helps in cases of cramp, glandular disorder and arterio-sclerosis. Many herbalists go further and affirm that the plant has rejuvenating properties from which old people generally can benefit. Similar qualities are attributed to Iceland moss (*Cetraria islandica*) which, like sundew, is also an efficient chest herb.

One teaspoonful of herb should be infused in a cup of sweetened water and taken daily.

TANSY
Tanacetum vulgare
Family: *Compositae*

Tansy flourishes in waste places and at roadsides, where it can be recognized by its feathery leaves and clusters of bright yellow flowers. The plant grows to a height of two to three feet, and was once a valued pot herb. It is still used by gipsies for culinary as well as medicinal purposes.

TANSY *Tanacetum vulgare*

Of the latter, the most remarkable is the herb's effect on the circulation, which it improves considerably. It is also invaluable in treating varicose veins. A teaspoonful of herb should be infused in a cupful of water, and the liquid drunk twice daily or applied externally to varicose veins, bruises, sties and minor swellings. Some herbalists regard tansy as a general tonic and also as a remedy for poor appetite, jaundice and certain forms of dropsy.

A relation of tansy is the common garden herb goose tongue (*Tanacetum balsamita*), often known as costmary. Its long, broad, light-green leaves are either eaten raw or used to prepare a standard infusion which is a liver and general tonic.

THISTLE
Family: *Compositae*

Thistles flourish on waste ground, in pastures and along most country hedgerows. Their thick prickly stems, lance-like leaves and purple flower-heads will be familiar to all (see p. 8o).

All thistles come under the benign influence of Jupiter, and so are noteworthy for their tonic effect on the liver and blood. They stimulate the circulation, banish sluggishness and promote a pleasing sense of well-being. Make an infusion using one and a half ounces of herb (leaves and chopped stalk) to half a pint of water. Take a wineglassful daily.

The holy or milk thistle (*Silybum marianum*) is a fine health-giver and anti-depressant, and has a tonic effect on the heart, brain and kidneys. It is said to restore a memory impaired by old age or sickness. The preparation and dosages are the same.

THYME *Thymus serpyllum*

THYME
Thymus serpyllum (wild thyme),
Thymus vulgaris (garden thyme)
Family: *Labiatae*

Thyme grows wild on dry banks and heaths. It has woody stems, covered in fine hair, and flattish, round leaves, growing in pairs. The flowers are borne in whorls and, like the rest of the plant, are heavily scented. This herb has been cultivated for centuries for use in both cookery and medicine.

The medicinal uses of thyme derive firstly from its cleansing properties. (An oil of thyme was once a standard ingredient of most antiseptic lotions and commercial disinfectants.) A poultice can be made from the leaves that will combat all forms of inflammation and infection. Taken internally (standard infusion), thyme is a first-rate digestive, febrifuge and liver tonic. Anti-spasmodic and nervine, it is held to cure a wide range of psychological disorders, including even insanity. Headaches, hysteria, halitosis and assorted female ailments (especially mastitis) are but a few of the other varied conditions for which this precious herb is traditionally prescribed.

TOADFLAX *Linaria vulgaris*

TOADFLAX
Linaria vulgaris
Family: *Scrophulariaceae*
Toadflax grows in pastures, waste places and, as an intruder, in fields of corn and other cereal crops. At the height of summer it has deep yellow flowers shaped rather like snapdragon flowers.

A powerful dissolvent, this herb, taken as a standard infusion (leaves and chopped stalk), removes gravelly deposits and similar obstructions from the bladder and kidneys. It is an important lymph tonic, and possibly the best cure for jaundice. An ointment containing toadflax and lesser celandine is a standard botanical treatment for haemorrhoids.

TWITCH
Agropyron repens   Family: *Gramineae*
Also known as couch grass, this prolific weed is found almost everywhere. It has long coarse leaves and roots that descend from tough, white runners.

An efficient dissolvent of gravelly deposits, twitch is prescribed for gall stones and disorders of the bladder. It also benefits inflamed or partly calcified kidneys. The same herb is a competent liver tonic and will cure mild forms of jaundice. It is both laxative and vermifuge.

A standard infusion is generally made from the leaves and root runners (both chopped first). For taste, add some rosemary or thyme and sweeten the mixture. A cupful night and morning is advisable, but should this prove too laxative, reduce the dosage.

VALERIAN
Valeriana officinalis   Family: *Valerianaceae*
A native of damp woods and riversides, valerian (see p. 80) is a tallish plant with clusters of pink or, less commonly, white flowers. This plant

has a curious effect on some animals – cats become frisky on smelling it, and an oil prepared from valerian and aniseed is used by gipsies to quell unfriendly dogs. Horses, too, are known to like its scent, as are rats and mice, for whose benefit it was once used as a bait in traps.

One of the most widely used nerve tonics, valerian has a relaxing and even euphoric effect on the system, although too much of it brings about the opposite result. To obtain the maximum benefit, take a tablespoonful of a decoction from the root of the plant or a teaspoonful of the fresh juice daily. The latter is often prescribed as a cure for insomnia, where its great value is that it calms the mind without having a narcotic effect.

VERVAIN
Verbena officinalis Family: *Verbenaceae*
Not a spectacular plant, having sparse, greeny-grey leaves and small hooded mauve flowers (see p. 80). Even so, vervain has a sound religious and magical pedigree, for it is the divine weed that was sprinkled on the altars of Jupiter, the *herba veneris* employed in rites of love and a sacred plant of the Druids. Latter-day magicians wear a crown of vervain as protection during the evocation of demons.

For centuries vervain has led the botanical field in the treatment of nervous disorders, epilepsy and asthma. It also fortifies the liver, heart and spleen, relieves mental strain and helps cure infectious diseases. (A wineglassful of a standard infusion, made from the flowers, leaves and diced stalk, should be taken on rising.) The infusion may be used as a gargle or mouth-wash for sore throats and gums or as an eye lotion of considerable merit.

Albertus Magnus calls this herb 'pisterion', and recommends it for curing inflammation and diseases of the skin. It is an efficient vermifuge.

VIOLET
Viola odorata and *Viola canina* Family: *Violaceae*
Found on sunny banks, in woods and along hedgerows, 'half hidden from the eye', the violet has heart-shaped leaves and, in the spring, sweetly scented flowers of various shades from blue to white.

In spite of its shy appearance, the violet is one of nature's most powerful dissolvents, being widely used in the treatment of internal

obstructions such as 'stones' and 'gravel'. (It will also tackle swollen glands, tumours, goitres and boils, particularly if the treatment is supplemented by the external application of an ointment or poultice composed of pulped leaves.) The same herb calms the nerves, quickens the intellect and will cure pleurisy. It is certainly a first-rate chest herb, being strongly decongestant and expectorant. It is also strengthening to the heart, and is frequently used in Switzerland to treat angina pectoris. A tisane of the leaves quickly dispels headaches.

For an infusion of this plant, combine two teaspoonfuls of its leaves with a breakfastcupful of water. For external use, where appropriate, prepare a standard infusion for use as a lotion.

VIPER'S BUGLOSS
Echium vulgare   Family: *Boraginaceae*
Wherever there is chalky soil, as at roadsides and on wasteland, viper's bugloss will generally be found (see p. 80). Its leaves grow directly from the stem and its cyme bears red and blue flowers.

Most headaches, but nervous ones especially, are speedily relieved by drinking a tisane prepared from this herb (leaves and stem). Taken as an infusion, it has a salutary effect on the nervous system, and a decoction of the seeds in claret will uplift the spirit. According to Homer, Helen of Troy used this herb (*nepenthe*) to cheer up the guests at a dinner party given by Menelaus.

WATERCRESS
Nasturtium officinale   Family: *Cruciferae*
Watercress grows in streams and springs, flourishing best where there is pure running water. It has dark green leaves and tiny white flowers. Although it is still possible to gather wild watercress, it is best bought from a greengrocer whenever there is some doubt concerning its identity or the purity of the water in which it lives.

Because of its nicely sharp taste, watercress is a popular salad herb.

A tonic one, too, since its leaves are full of minerals, especially iron. As a result it has always been used to treat anaemia. It has antiseptic properties, also: the raw seeds – one dessertspoonful on an empty stomach – will cleanse the system and rid it of worms when these are present. Herbalists make much use of this herb, for example in treating stiffness, cramps and all rheumatic pains. It will also improve the eyes, the nerves and the heart. Above all, however, I have found watercress to be a reliable dissolver of all cysts, swellings and tumours. It is this ability which has doubtless led some herbalists to use it in the treatment of cancer. (It is employed on its own during the primary stage and with other herbs when the disease is more advanced.)

Eat as much as possible of the fresh herb.

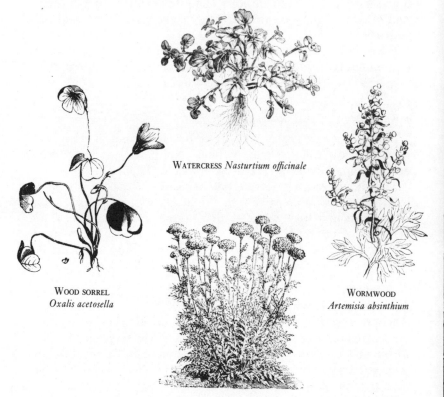

WATERCRESS *Nasturtium officinale*

WOOD SORREL
Oxalis acetosella

WORMWOOD
Artemisia absinthium

YARROW *Achillea millefolium*

Wood Sorrel

Oxalis acetosella   Family: *Oxalidaceae*

A delicate woodland plant whose trefoil leaves are mauve-backed and have a tendency to droop when rain or darkness threatens. The chewed leaves are a refreshing thirst-quencher, their pleasant tartness deriving from the oxalic acid they contain. The white flowers are comparatively large and grow singly on long slender stalks.

Wood sorrel is a tonic for the liver and blood, a remedy for disorders of the kidneys and bladder and a cure for diseases of the genital glands. Eat half a handful of raw leaves or prepare a standard infusion.

Wormwood

Artemisia absinthium   Family: *Compositae*

A perennial aromatic plant that grows at roadsides and on wastes, wormwood has fringed grey-green leaves and small yellow flowers.

This herb has been used since classical times to treat all ailments of the digestive system: constipation, enteritis and common indigestion. Wormwood also cures jaundice, kidney disorders and most female complaints, in addition to being a valuable tonic. It is a bitter plant, so sweeten the infusion (made from the young leaves and flowers). In all cases two tablespoonfuls should be swallowed night and morning until no longer needed.

Yarrow

Achillea millefolium   Family: *Compositae*

A familiar plant on commons, in fields and along the sides of country lanes, yarrow has greyish, feathery, ethereal-looking leaves, and, from early summer onwards, clusters of small daisy-like flowers. Yarrow was one of the witch herbs, and it was believed that carrying it at weddings guaranteed seven years of married bliss. (Then the seven-year itch presumably set in.)

Yarrow has been used since antiquity for headaches, fevers and influenza. It will also curb diarrhoea, palpitations and excessive menstruation. The sufferer should take one wineglassful night and morning of a standard infusion prepared from the leaves and occasional flowers.

INDEX OF AILMENTS AND
THEIR HERBAL TREATMENT

Several different herbs are listed under many of the general headings given below. To ensure that you select the most suitable herb for your particular condition, you should always refer to the main text. The entry 'Kidneys', for example, lists as many as eighteen herbs; some are renal tonics, some dissolvents, while others treat specific conditions like renal inflammation. The entry 'Tonic' is equally wide-ranging, and includes, in addition to herbs that are general tonics, other plants which have a tonic effect on a particular organ. In all such cases a glance at the relevant pages should enable you to choose the herb or herbs you really need.

Abortion, threatened: feverfew, 106–7; raspberry, 133–4; strawberry, 143–4

Abrasions: centaury, 95; houndstongue, 117–18

Acne: betony, 86; birch, 87; *see also* 45 *and* Skin

Alopecia, *see* Scalp

Anaemia: blackberry, 87; peppermint, 126; spearmint, 126; strawberry, 143–4; watercress, 149–50; *see also* 37

Analgesic herbs: betony, 86; catnip, 93; cinquefoil, 97–8; cowslip, 101; feverfew, 106–7; figwort, 107; horsetail, 117; lavender, 120; mignonette, 125; mullein, 127–8; red clover, 134–5; St John's wort, 35, 138–9; stinking iris, 143

Angina pectoris, *see* Heart

Antiseptic herbs: golden rod, 110–11; horse radish, 116–17; marigold, 123; nasturtium, 128; thyme, 146–7; watercress, 149–50

Appetite, poor: gentian, 110; knapweed, 119; mint, 126; tansy, 145

Apoplexy, *see* Seizure

Arteriosclerosis: daisy, 101–2; hawthorn, 112–13; hazel, 113; mistletoe, 126–7; rue, 137–8; sundew, 144–5; *see also* 43

Arthritis: burdock, 90; candytuft, 92–3; cleavers, 98; dandelion, 102–3; honeysuckle, 115; primrose, 133; *see also* 44

Ascites, *see* Dropsy

Asthma: elecampane, 104–5; garlic, 109–10; heartsease, 113–14; honeysuckle, 115; mullein, 127–8; plantain, 132; poppy, 132–3; speedwell, 142–3; vervain, 148

Biliousness: centaury, 95; fumitory, 108–9; gentian, 110; sage, 138

Bladder: barley, 85; cleavers, 98; golden rod, 110–11; parsley, 130; toadflax, 147;

twitch, 147; violet, 148–9; wood sorrel, 151; *see also* 43

Bleeding, *see* Haemorrhage

Blisters: St John's wort, 138–9; *see also* Skin

Blood: barley, 85; betony, 86; burdock, 90; burnet, 90–91; garlic, 109–10; gentian, 110; meadowsweet, 124–5; nasturtium, 128; sorrel, 142; strawberry, 143–4; thistle, 145–6; watercress, 149–50; wood sorrel, 151; *see also* 45

Blood pressure, high: figwort, 107; hyssop, 118; meadowsweet, 124–5; primrose, 133; rosemary, 136–7; *see also* 45

Blood pressure, low: dandelion, 102–3; hyssop, 118; lady's mantle, 45

Boils: houndstongue, 117–18; lesser celandine, 94; sorrel, 142; violet, 148–9; *see also* Skin

Brain: chervil, 95–6; garlic, 109–10; holy thistle, 146; lily-of-the-valley, 120–21; rose, 135–6; sage, 138

Bronchitis: nettle, 129; plantain, 132; speedwell, 142–3; *see also* Coughs

Bruising: comfrey, 99–100; daisy, 101–2; feverfew, 106–7; houndstongue, 117–18; houseleek, 118; hyssop, 118; tansy, 145

Burns: elder, 104; *see also* Skin

Cancer: cleavers, 98; parsley, 130; red clover, 134–5; watercress, 149–50

Cardiac disorder, *see* Heart

Catarrh: blackcurrant, 87–8; elder, 103–4; elecampane, 104–5; ground ivy, 112; horsetail, 117; houndstongue, 117–18; hyssop, 118; knapweed, 119; marigold, 123; mullein, 127–8; poppy, 132–3; rose, 135–6; sanicle, 139; speedwell, 142–3

Change of life, *see* Menopause

Chilblains: chestnut, 96; daisy, 101–2; snowdrop, 141–2

Chorea: devil's bit scabious, 103; skullcap, 141; stinking iris, 143

Circulation, poor: chestnut, 96; daisy, 101–2; dandelion, 102–3; figwort, 107; marigold, 123; mistletoe, 126–7; nettle, 129; peppermint, 126; spearmint, 126; tansy, 145; thistle, 145–6

Colds: elder, 103–4; honeysuckle, 115; horehound, 116; sage, 138; yarrow, 151

Conjunctivitis, *see* Eye disorders

Constipation, *see* Laxative herbs

Convulsions, *see* Chorea *and* Epilepsy

Coughs:* agrimony, 82; blackcurrant, 87–8; catnip, 93; coltsfoot, 98–9; elder, 103–4; elecampane, 104–5; fennel, 105–6; garlic, 109–10; ground ivy, 112; honeysuckle, 115; horehound, 116; houndstongue, 117–18; hyssop, 118; lavender, 120; lime, 121; marshmallow, 123–4; nettle, 129; rosemary, 136–7; sage, 138; sundew, 144–5; violet, 148–9

Cramp: fennel, 105–6; fumitory, 108–9; rue, 137–8; sundew, 144–5; watercress, 149–50

Cyst: watercress, 149–50; *see also* Boils

Cystitis, *see* Bladder

Dandruff: cleavers, 98; *see also* Scalp *and* 53

Dental disorder: seakale, 140; strawberry, 143–4

Depression: bog myrtle, 88–9; chervil, 95–6; heather, 114; holy thistle, 146;

---

* Some of the following herbs are decongestant and expectorant, which means they should be taken when there is phlegm to be lifted from the chest. Others have a sedative effect, and will thus check unproductive coughs. There is, of course, no point in taking both sorts together.

nettle, 129; pimpernel, 131; valerian, 147–8; viper's bugloss, 149; *see also* 39, 43

Dermatitis, *see* Skin

Diabetes: meadowsweet, 124–5; periwinkle, 130–31

Diarrhoea: blackberry, 87–8; horsetail, 117; meadowsweet, 124–5; sea lavender, 140–41; shepherd's purse, 47; strawberry, 143–4; wormwood, 151; yarrow, 151

Disinfectant herbs, *see* Antiseptic herbs

Diuretic herbs, *see* Bladder *and* Kidneys

Dropsy: alder, 82; broom, 89; dwarf elder, 104; honeysuckle, 115; horse radish, 116–17; ivy, 118–19; lily-of-the-valley, 120–21; pimpernel, 131; tansy, 145

Dyspepsia, *see* Indigestion

Ear disorders: houseleek, 118

Eczema: birch, 87; horehound, 116; speedwell, 142–3; strawberry, 143–4; *see also* Skin

Enteritis: meadowsweet, 124–5; sea lavender, 140–41; *see also* Diarrhoea

Epilepsy: cinquefoil, 97–8; devil's bit scabious, 103; heartsease, 113–14; skullcap, 141; stinking iris, 143; vervain, 148

Erysipelas: houseleek, 118; *see also* Skin

Eye disorders: comfrey, 99–100; cornflower, 100–101; eyebright, 121; fennel, 105–6; greater celandine, 94; groundsel, 97; houseleek, 118; lady's mantle, 94 n; loosestrife, 121; lovage, 94 n; mugwort, 94 n; pimpernel, 131; speedwell, 142–3; vervain, 148; watercress, 149–50

Feet, tired: alder, 82

Female disorders: balm, 83–4; camomile, 92; coriander, 100; devil's bit scabious, 103; feverfew, 106–7; raspberry, 133–4; rose, 135–6; thyme, 146–7; wormwood, 151; *see also* 45–6

Fever, balm, 83–4; cleavers, 98; coltsfoot, 95–9; golden rod, 110–11; hyssop, 118; ivy, 118–19; lavender, 120; sage, 138; sea lavender, 140–41; strawberry, 143–4; yarrow, 151

Fibrositis, *see* Analgesic herbs, Muscles *and* Rheumatism

Fingernails, brittle: horsetail, 117

Flatulence, *see* Indigestion

Fractures: comfrey, 99–100; boneset, 99

Freckles: daisy, 101–2; pimpernel, 131

Frostbite: snowdrop, 141–2

Gall bladder: eyebright, 105; toadflax, 147; twitch, 147; violet, 148–9

Gangrene: golden rod, 110–11

Gastric disorder, *see* Indigestion

Genital disorders: golden seal, 111

Giddiness: hawthorn, 112–13

Gingivitis, *see* Gum disorders

Glands: borage, 89; ground ivy, 112; honeysuckle, 115; ivy, 118–19; knapweed, 119; red clover, 134–5; sea holly, 139–40; sundew, 144–5; violet, 148–9; wood sorrel, 151

Goitre: houndstongue, 117–18; reed, 135; violet, 148–9

Gout: meadow saffron, 124

Gum disorders: lavender, 120; sage, 138; seakale, 140; vervain, 148; *see also* 46

Haemorrhage: burnet, 90–91; golden rod, 110–11; horsetail, 117; mullein, 127–8; nettle, 129; oak, 129–30; St John's wort, 138–9; sea lavender, 140–41; strawberry, 143–4

Haemorrhoids: chestnut, 96; feverfew, 106–7; lesser celandine, 94; stonecrop, 94; toadflax, 147

Hair: camomile, 92; lime, 121; maidenhair fern, 122; pimpernel, 131; rosemary, 136–7; *see also* 53

Halitosis: lavender, 120; thyme, 146–7

Hay fever: mullein, 127–8; poppy, 132–3

Headache: betony, 86; foxglove, 107–8; lavender, 120; mignonette, 125; red clover, 135; sage, 138; stinking iris, 143; thyme, 146–7; violet, 148–9; viper's bugloss, 149; *see also* Analgesic herbs

Heart: borage, 89; butterbur, 91; coriander, 100; figwort, 107; foxglove, 107–8; hawthorn, 112–13; hazel, 113; heartsease, 113–14; holy thistle, 146; honeysuckle, 115; lily-of-the-valley, 120–21; maidenhair fern, 122; mistletoe, 126–7; rose, 135–6; rosemary, 136–7; vervain, 148; *see also* 43

Hepatitis, *see* Jaundice

Hiccups: catnip, 93

Hysteria: cinquefoil, 97–8; devil's bit scabious, 103; stinking iris, 143; thyme, 146–7

Impotence: hazel, 113; mint, 126; raspberry, 133–4

Indigestion: angelica, 83; basil, 85–6; borage, 89; bugle, 89–90; camomile, 92; catnip, 93; chickweed, 97; coriander, 100; eyebright, 105; fennel, 105–6; feverfew, 106–7; fumitory, 108–9; gentian, 110; golden rod, 110–11; ground ivy, 112; hyssop, 118; lucerne, 122; meadowsweet, 124–5; mint, 126; nasturtium, 128; periwinkle, 130–31; plantain, 132; rose, 135–6; rosemary, 136–7; speedwell, 142–3; strawberry, 143–4; thyme, 146–7; wormwood, 151

Infertility: balm, 83–4; feverfew, 106–7; skullcap, 141; *see also* 45–6

Inflammation: feverfew, 106–7; foxglove, 107–8; golden seal, 111; hyssop, 118; lavender, 120; marshmallow, 123–4; nettle, 129; pimpernel, 131; plantain, 132; poppy, 132–3; sanicle, 139; thyme, 146–7

Influenza, *see* Colds, Headache, Throat, *etc.*

Insomnia, *see* Sedative herbs *and* Soporific herbs

Iritis, *see* Eye disorders

Jaundice: borage, 89; centaury, 95; cleavers, 98; golden rod, 110–11; parsley, 130; pimpernel, 131; sorrel, 142; tansy, 145; toadflax, 147; twitch, 147; wormwood, 151

Kidneys: alder, 82; barley, 85; borage, 89; butterbur, 91; dandelion, 102–3; golden rod, 110–11; holy thistle, 146; horse radish, 116–17; horsetail, 117; lucerne, 122; nettle, 129; parsley, 130; sorrel, 142; toadflax, 147; twitch, 147; violet, 148–9; wood sorrel, 151; wormwood, 151; *see also* 43

Laxative herbs: blackberry, 87; elder, 103–4; fennel, 105–6; feverfew, 106–7; groundsel, 97; horehound, 116; sea holly, 139–40; seakale, 140; twitch, 147; wormwood, 151; *see also* 46–7

Liver: agrimony, 82; barberry, 84; centaury, 95; dandelion, 101–3; fumitory, 108–9; gentian, 110; honeysuckle, 115; horsetail, 117; maidenhair fern, 122; rosemary, 136–7; sage, 138; sea holly, 139–40; sorrel, 142; strawberry, 143–4; thistle, 145–6; thyme, 146–7; twitch, 147; vervain, 148; wood sorrel, 151

Lungs: elecampane, 104–5; garlic, 109–10; *see also* Coughs *and* Pleurisy

Lymph: broom, 89; lily-of-the-valley, 120–21; reed, 135; toadflax, 147

Melancholia, *see* Depression

Memory, poor: bog myrtle, 88–9; chervil, 95–6; fennel, 105–6; holy thistle, 146; sage, 138

Menopause: raspberry, 133–4

Menstrual disorder: balm, 83–4; catnip, 93; oak, 129–30; raspberry, 133–4;

rosemary, 136–7; strawberry, 143–4; yarrow, 151

Migraine, see Analgesic herbs, Headache

Milk, over-copious (nursing mothers): borage, 89; milkwort, 89

Milk, inadequate (nursing mothers): periwinkle, 130–31

Morning sickness: basil, 85–6; golden rod, 110–11

Muscles, painful, etc.: ivy, 118–19; lavender, 120; meadow saffron, 124

Narcotic herbs: see Soporific herbs *and* Chapter 6

Nausea: basil, 85–6; fumitory, 108–9; gentian, 110; golden rod, 110–11; red clover, 135

Nephritis, see Kidneys

Nerves: balm, 83–4; barley, 85; basil, 85–6; betony, 86; bog myrtle, 88–9; catnip, 93; cinquefoil, 97–8; cornflower, 100–101; devil's bit scabious, 103; gentian, 110; heather, 114; hyssop, 118; lavender, 120; lily-of-the-valley, 120–21; lime, 121; mignonette, 125; mistletoe, 126–7; nasturtium, 128; raspberry, 133–4; rosemary, 136–7; sage, 138; St John's wort, 138–9; sea holly, 139–40; skullcap, 141; strawberry, 143–4; thyme, 146–7; valerian, 147–8; vervain, 148; violet, 148–9; viper's bugloss, 149; watercress, 149–50; see also 43

Neuralgia: betony, 86; red clover, 135; see also Analgesic herbs

Nightmares: betony, 86; rosemary, 136–7; see also Sedative herbs

Obesity, see 46, 55

Ophthalmic disorders, see Eye disorders

Paralysis: cornflower, 100–101; lavender, 120

Piles, see Haemorrhoids

Pimples: dandelion, 102–3; mistletoe,

126–7; see also Acne, Skin

Pleurisy: marshmallow, 123–4; mullein, 127–8; poppy, 132–3; violet, 148–9

Pruritis: birch, 87; speedwell, 142–3; strawberry, 143–4; see also Skin

Psoriasis: blackberry, 87; see also Skin

Psychological disorders: sage, 138; thyme, 146–7; vervain, 148; see also Depression, Memory, Nerves, *etc.*

Rashes, see Skin

Rheumatism: agrimony, 82; birch, 87; burdock, 90; candytuft, 92–3; elecampane, 104–5; fennel, 105–6; garlic, 109–10; honeysuckle, 115; mint, 126; parsley, 130; primrose, 133; rue, 137–8; seakale, 140; watercress, 149–50; see also Analgesic herbs

Ringworm: borage, 89; houseleek, 118

Scalds: elder, 103–4; St John's wort, 138–9; see also Skin

Scalp: burdock, 90; cleavers, 98; lime, 121; maidenhair fern, 122; periwinkle, 130–31

Sciatica: burdock, 90; parsley, 130; rue, 137–8

Sedative herbs: basil, 85–6; bugle, 89–90; camomile, 92; cinquefoil, 97–8; cowslip, 101; ground ivy, 112; heartsease, 113–14; lily-of-the-valley, 120–21; mullein, 127–8; skullcap, 141

Seizure: cornflower, 100–101; fennel, 105–6; lily-of-the-valley, 120–21; lavender, 120

Senility: bog myrtle, 88–9; chervil, 95–6; holy thistle, 146; Iceland moss, 145; sundew, 144–5; see also 39

Shingles: horehound, 116; horsetail, 117

Sight, poor or failing: eyebright, 105; loosestrife, 121; nasturtium, 128; speedwell, 142–3

Sinusitis, see Catarrh

Skin, herbs for the: blackberry, 87; burdock, 90; burnet, 90–91; camomile,